"This book certainly belongs in every American law library. However, this work goes well beyond the law; the story of bourbon is the story of America's history. Any reader with an interest in our past will enjoy this excellent book about a wonderful beverage that has had an important effect on our nation."
—MARK W. PODVIA, *Criminal Law and Criminal Justice Books*

"Brian Haara tells us the fascinating story of how many very litigious bourbon folks ended up, often accidentally, crafting a new and different American commercial society that is still with us today. Lawsuits that started with bourbon ended up affecting industries as far reaching as women's lingerie and mouthwash."
—ERIC BURKE, *Bourbon Guy*

"A fun read for those who like bourbon, justice, American history, or American legal history."
—CHARLES DRESOW, Marin County Bar Association

"I teach people all over the world that words on an American whiskey label mean something. Brian Haara brings to life the laws like the Bottled-in-Bond Act of 1897 that make American whiskey so spectacular. I can't get enough!"
—BERNIE LUBBERS, American whiskey ambassador for Heaven Hill Distillery and author of Bourbon *Whiskey: Our Native Spirit*

"A very enjoyable read. Who knew that reading about law cases could actually be interesting?"
—*New Bourbon Drinker*

"This is not just another Bourbon 101 book; it's for those who really crave knowledge about how bourbon 'grew up' with America and is inexorably intertwined with our legal system today. . . . This book is the authority on how bourbon law shaped America."
—BILL STRAUB, *Modern Th*

BOURBON JUSTICE

BOURBON
JUSTICE

HOW WHISKEY LAW SHAPED AMERICA

BRIAN F. HAARA

FOREWORD BY FRED MINNICK

Potomac Books

AN IMPRINT OF THE UNIVERSITY OF NEBRASKA PRESS

Library of Congress Cataloging-in-Publication Data
Names: Haara, Brian F., author.
Title: Bourbon justice: how whiskey law shaped America /
Brian F. Haara; Foreword by Fred Minnick.
Description: Lincoln: Potomac Books, an imprint of
the University of Nebraska Press, 2018. | Includes
bibliographical references and index.
Identifiers: LCCN 2018006600
ISBN 9781640120853 (cloth: alk. paper)
ISBN 9781640124271 (paperback)
ISBN 9781640121294 (epub)
ISBN 9781640121300 (mobi)
ISBN 9781640121317 (pdf)
Subjects: LCSH: Liquor laws—United States—History. |
Bourbon whiskey—United States—History.
Classification: LCC KF3924.W45 H33 2018 |
DDC 344.7305/41—dc23 LC record available at
https://lccn.loc.gov/2018006600

Set in Garamond Premier Pro by E. Cuddy.

*Dad, I wish that we could
share another bourbon*

CONTENTS

ILLUSTRATIONS

FOREWORD

FRED MINNICK

Whiskey runs deep in our country's history.

It joined our troops on the field of battle, as Gen. George Washington made sure his soldiers had ample amounts for medicinal purposes. Many of those soldiers were whiskey makers, as was Washington, who, after winning the Revolutionary War, opted to tax distillers to pay for war debts. Naturally, many distillers cared not for this tax. And they did what all good 1790s protesters did: they tarred and feathered the opposition—a taxman. That led to the Whisky Rebellion, in which Washington federalized soldiers to thwart tax-hating whiskey rebels.

That wasn't the only time whiskey enters fabric of government and society.

When President Thomas Jefferson took office, he repealed the whiskey tax and later signed the Louisiana Purchase, opening the door to trade for distillers, who built empires in Kentucky. Bourbon distillers created one of America's first true industries, establishing jobs and dictating government regulation, such as the Bottled-in-Bond Act of 1897, Pure Food and Drug Act and the 1964 congressional declaration that gave bourbon its de facto moniker America's Spirit. Presidents Lincoln, Grant, Cleveland, Taft, Roosevelt, Kennedy, and Obama have benefited from the ever-growing bourbon business and helped establish bourbon law and popularity.

Whether you realize it, bourbon has influenced your life, too, through taxes—about 60 percent of every bottle goes to taxes; through branding, before Nike and McDonald's, bourbon branded themselves as "Old Crow," "Old Taylor," and "Old Grand-Dad"; and the courtroom, as we learn in this brilliant tome, *Bourbon Justice*.

In past bourbon histories, including my own, authors typically cover the men and women behind the brands, legislative hallmarks, and the occasional lawsuit. Longtime bourbon blogger and attorney Brian Haara covers it all through the courtroom, a fascinating place to study the American perspective of anything.

When business titans expand, create value, and innovate, they eventually sue one another.

Yeah, that's kind of the American way: land of the free, home of the brave and the litigious. As one of the country's first true industries, bourbon apparently played a much larger role in our court system than we had previously known. In *Bourbon Justice* Haara rips open the legal continuum and shows bourbon set precedent in all sorts of legal drama.

From the moment bourbon became popular, brands found themselves crossing into the courtroom, arguing trademark rights, property complaints and criminal activity. In writing several bourbon books, I found lawsuits to be a great source of information. But admittedly, I'm not a lawyer and sometimes didn't know the merits or significance of these cases outside of bourbon.

With its focus on an industry so entrenched in nepotism, *Bourbon Justice* studies a common problem in American business: what happens when a family member breaks away from the business to start their own company? Turns out, bourbon provided early arguments for both sides in this issue that comes down to previous agreements and what was previously allowed under the name. If you want to use your family name to start your own business, you may want to use the "Dant" argument, offering evidence your name is you and can be unique enough to not confuse consumers. Or if you want to protect your family name from family members, you may consider the Whiskey Trust's "unfair" trademark infringement argument after it purchased the Wathen name and brands and then sued the Wathens when they turned around and started R. E. Wathen & Company.

The book is filled with fascinating tidbits, such as the many lawsuits between George T. Stagg and E. H. Taylor, two iconic names that shaped the bourbon world. From the Churchill Downs lawsuit, where the famous racetrack sued the attempted Churchill Downs Distilling Company, to the Maker's Mark's red dripping wax case, in which a judge ruled nobody else should use a red dripping wax in alcohol, Haara masterfully intertwines bourbon law with the bourbon culture and mainstream courts. Did you know that bourbon law set the framework for a current-day lawsuit involving Victoria's Secret? Or that 1800s-era bourbon trademark disputes helped shape the trademark laws of America?

Like judges in between cases, Haara pours into a good bourbon to break up the legal briefings. I highly recommend sipping on the elixir he recommends to see if they pair well with the American legal system.

Of course, this isn't a tasting guide per se or a cocktail lifestyle book. It's an important bourbon history book that skews part scholarly effort, part narrative, and all bourbon.

But let me be clear: I cannot express how important this book is to bourbon history. We have needed this book.

As bourbon becomes more popular, we see more fluff and marketing passed off as history. Independent works like Haara's protect the true, unbiased identity of bourbon and offer us real depictions of America's spirit. Bourbon, now intertwined in our lives, has reached epic status of Americana, and the brands are as much ours as they are the companies who own them. We garner special affection for the category, travel long distances to hear distillers speak, and are willing to stand in long lines to get our favorite brands. You'll find many fans who permanently tattoo their favorite brands on their bodies or name their firstborns after distillers.

We love bourbon; it's in our blood; it's who we are. If anybody tries to take bourbon away from us, by god, we'll sue, using this book as precedent. And Brian Haara will be our lawyer.

The Squire

If one would know the real Bluegrass charm,
He first must stop at Winburn Farm
And meet the Squire.
Nobody here is ever bored,
Gray shadows dance on Morgan's sword
Above the fire.

The Squire leans back among his books,
Pioneers emerge from leafy nooks
With powder horn.
"Let's talk of Boone and Clark," he'll say,
"Zac Taylor, too, at Monterey,
And sip our corn."

—WILLIAM H. TOWNSEND

"The Squire" was dedicated by Kentucky attorney, poet, and Civil War scholar William H. Townsend to his friend J. Winston Coleman Jr., also known as "the Squire." The bluegrass charm that it evokes is tied to Kentucky history along with America's native spirit— bourbon. The two are inexorably intertwined in Kentucky.

While bourbon tracks the history of our developing nation, *bourbon law* similarly tracks the history of the development of American law. The Squire might have told some of the stories that you are about to read along with his tales about Boone, Clark, and Taylor, so please enjoy, possibly while you sip your corn.

BOURBON JUSTICE

ONE

Bourbon History Tells the Story of American History

Bourbon and law might seem, to the casual observer, to be connected only in negative ways: Prohibition, illegal stills, and organized crime. While nostalgic in many respects, those connections focus on lawlessness. Lawlessness, however, is the mere tip of the proverbial iceberg for bourbon—the real history of bourbon, hidden beneath the surface, is the foundation of American commercial law and its relation to American history as a whole. Indeed, bourbon *justice* tells the history of America through the development of commercial laws, guiding our nation from an often reckless laissez-faire mentality, through the growing pains of industrialization, past the overcorrection of Prohibition, and into the tranquility of finally becoming a nation of laws.

American history and bourbon history have each told their separate stories, occasionally intertwined, but never have their connected stories been told exclusively through lawsuits. So much of bourbon history has been lost, sometimes because records and accounts were not kept and other times because records and accounts were swept away during Prohibition. Distillers from the 1800s and early 1900s did not trouble themselves with memorializing their craft for anyone other than a son or apprentice, and first-person accounts are rare. Because of this lack of traditional historical evidence, lawsuits are an abundant resource not just for information but for *facts* that satisfied rigorous evidentiary standards or withstood the pressure of cross-examination and were found to be reliable. Lawsuits might be the best source of facts. That is why, with only a few exceptions, every source cited in *Bourbon Justice* is a lawsuit, statute, or regulation.

But why use bourbon law to tell American history? Arguably, no single commodity has contributed more to the development of American legal history than bourbon. Therefore, bourbon and bourbon law trace the development of the United States as a nation, from conquering the wild frontier to rugged individualism to fostering the entrepreneurial spirit to establishing a nation of laws. Bourbon—and whiskey more generally—helped shape the growth and maturation of many substantive areas of the law, like trademark, breach of contract, fraud, governmental regulation and taxation, and consumer protection.

Why not use brandy, rum, or even wine, which all predate bourbon, to tell this story? Not only do these other spirits and wine fail to have a meaningful presence in American legal history; none of them are distinctively American.[1] Only bourbon can claim that title; it is distinctively—and legally—American. Congress did not officially recognize this distinctiveness until 1964, but bourbon had certainly been uniquely American since the first drop of majority-corn distillate was barrel aged. Bourbon is distinctively American because Americans are often celebrated as entrepreneurial mavericks. Historically, we have aspired to greatness, we have been ruggedly independent, we have been resourceful, and we have been highly competitive. Because of those characteristics, Americans have flouted the law when it was deemed necessary, lobbied for new consumer protection laws or self-interested protectionism laws, and strategically stretched and used laws to gain an advantage over the competition. Bourbon history covers each of these bases.

We Americans have also not been great fans of paying taxes. After winning a war over taxation without representation, farmer-distillers in Pennsylvania rebelled against the young nation's first internal tax,[2] and many scattered southwestward to the Kentucky frontier in 1794, where immigrants had already established themselves as Kentuckians and as distillers. Kentucky County, Virginia, had recently been formed in 1776, and the establishment of Fort Nelson in 1778 in present-day Louisville, followed by the city of Louisville in 1780, provided safety and a hub for wilderness and river commerce. With the end of the Revolutionary War and the Treaty of Paris in 1783, safe passage to Kentucky was a reality, and families like the Samuels, Beams, Hadens, and Wathens arrived. Statehood followed in 1792, and Kentucky was primed to be a whiskey-distilling powerhouse.

Freedom and survival—combined with bountiful natural resources, fertile soil, fresh limestone-filtered water, and perfect weather—proved to be the mother of bourbon. At its height reports claim that over two thousand farmers were also active distillers in Kentucky. Not only did whiskey provide a source of income for these farmers, but it also provided an exchange for barter transactions, it developed into a loose form of currency, and as transactions became more sophisticated, it served as a commodity backing negotiable instruments.

Over time these farmers with entrepreneurial spirit found it economical to distill on a larger scale, and then, of course, entire families joined the business, and investors provided capital for expansion. One of the earliest family dynasties was the Wathen family. Often relegated to footnotes today, members of the Wathen family were early whiskey pioneers, with Henry Hudson Wathen settling near Lebanon, Kentucky, in 1788 and starting a distillery by 1790. The second Wathen generation (Richard Bernard Wathen) built a bigger distillery, and his five sons each joined the distilling business. One of them, John Bernard Wathen, moved to Louisville to build the J. B. Wathen & Brother Distillery, one of the biggest distilleries of the time. Not only were the Wathens pioneers, but they also showed remarkable survival instincts and business savvy by forming the American Medicinal Spirits Company, which thrived during National Prohibition (January 1920–December 1933) and exited Prohibition as an industry leader. The Wathen family can tell the American dream story as well as anyone—each generation doing better than the previous one.

Some entrepreneurs bit off more than they could chew, like the Hope Distillery in Louisville, which was built between 1816 and 1817, with previously unheard-of capacity. Its 1,500-gallon and 750-gallon stills reportedly could produce over 1,200 gallons of whiskey per day. But the nation was not ready for this mass capacity, so the Hope Distillery failed and was abandoned by 1821. Other commercial distillers experienced wild success. But wild success was often accompanied by catastrophic losses. Even successful commercial distillers experienced the highs and the lows of the market, sometimes in less-than-honorable fashion. For instance, one of the most famous figures in bourbon history, Col. Edmund Haynes Taylor Jr., sold the same barrels twice in 1877 and had to physically leave Kentucky to avoid creditors.[3]

Throughout this time of boom and bust, however, bourbon and America were growing up together. The success of bourbon and American's insatiable thirst for whiskey opened the door for another American tradition: scammers. In a more charitable light or in their best incarnation, these entrepreneurs were just "innovating" to meet market demands, and some were even honest. In 1853 Pierre Lacour published *The Manufacture of Liquors, Wines and Cordials without the Aid of Distillation*, which contained a recipe for "Old Bourbon Whiskey" that blended neutral spirits, simple syrup, tea, oil of wintergreen, tincture of cochineal (a bug that when crushed provided red coloring), and burnt sugar. Similarly, in 1885 Joseph Fleischman published *The Art of Blending and Compounding Liquors and Wines*, which contained a variety of recipes that could be passed off as bourbon and rye, mostly involving neutral spirits, prune and other juices, tea, simple syrup, and coloring. Scammers could sell this "rectified" liquor as "bourbon."

There was also a dirty underbelly of rectifiers who used hazardous additives, including sulfuric acid.[4] Regardless of the methods, whiskey rectifying was big business. The Kentucky Court of Appeals, in *E. H. Taylor, Jr. & Sons Co. v. Marion E. Taylor*, even recognized that rectified or blended whiskey was more popular than straight whiskey.[5] Colonel Taylor was instrumental in changing that tide, running rectifiers out of town through relentless lawsuits, and in passing the Bottled-in-Bond Act of 1897—which, remarkably, was the nation's first consumer protection law.[6] When rectifiers persisted in misleading consumers even after passage of the act, President William Howard Taft took the unprecedented step, in 1909, of formally defining "straight," "blended," and "imitation" whiskey to further protect the public and to provide assurances that the public could know exactly what they were buying and drinking.

Both before and after the Bottled-in-Bond Act, straight bourbon whiskey gained some of its fame in part because of who drank it, perhaps showing that Americans have always had a fascination with celebrity trends. Various reports claim that Ulysses S. Grant, Henry Clay, and Mark Twain were avid bourbon fans, particularly of Old Crow. President Truman's morning routine reportedly involved a shot of bourbon. Many brands today still closely align themselves with celebrities (Wild Turkey and Matthew McConaughey or Jim Beam and Mila Kunis) or try a subtler approach of product placement (Bulleit in HBO's *Deadwood*).

No celebrity could prevent the drama of National Prohibition, which destroyed the farmer-distiller and small operations, consolidating ownership with a handful of industrialists, and turned much of bourbon's rich history into embarrassing family baggage. The most politically savvy and best-funded industrial distillers secured their futures with government-approved medicinal licensing. The rest of the distillers, without medicinal licenses, were mothballed or torn down.

After Repeal in 1933, however, bourbon was back at the forefront of developing law. America was in a new industrial age, and competition was fierce. Distilleries that had been shuttered and neglected during Prohibition were being renovated and fired up. New entrepreneurs and investors were looking for names that harked back to pre-Prohibition memories. The companies that survived Prohibition had an advantage both with production capacity and the all-important stock of aged whiskey, but the new "little guys" were nipping at their heels. Some of these new distillers, however, tried to use the names and goodwill of established brands to promote their new brands.[7]

The growing industry meant that the nation needed laws again, this time not so much for consumer protection but for business protection. Bourbon law led the charge with new developments in trademarks, trade names, and unfair competition law. Bourbon litigation clarified that trade names are protectable beyond just a company's line of business.[8] Bourbon litigation also clarified when a person could use a family surname or not.[9] And it strengthened truth-in-labeling laws that it had prompted in the 1800s.[10]

Bourbon's popularity subsided after it was designated as a distinctive product of the United States, and it hit rock bottom in the 1980s. Vodka and wine coolers ruled the day, and there was very little interest in bourbon. The historic Ancient Age Distillery (now Buffalo Trace) in Frankfort, Kentucky, was in danger of closing. It employed only fifty people in 1991, and despite the successful launch of Blanton's Single Barrel bourbon in 1984, things looked bleak. But the resurgence was practically around the corner for any distillery that could survive. Many, however, did not.

Heaven Hill Distillery set the groundwork for bourbon's turnaround in 1986 with its release of Elijah Craig 12 Year—the first "small batch" bourbon—named after the Baptist preacher credited through legend as the first distiller to age his whiskey in charred oak barrels. Later, in 1995, Heaven Hill helped revive appreciation for bottled in bond bourbon, with its release of Henry McKenna Bottled-in-Bond single barrel bourbon.

Louisville-based Brown-Forman Corporation, which traces its roots to 1870, when George Garvin Brown started J. T. S. Brown and Brother to sell Old Forester, also helped foster bourbon's rebirth when it repurchased a small, scenic distillery in Woodford County, Kentucky. In 1996 Brown-Forman introduced Woodford Reserve bourbon and reintroduced the world to the all-but-forgotten Labrot & Graham Distillery and the history of Oscar Pepper and James Crow.

Bourbon was staging a comeback, and a resurgence of litigation came with it to help shape current-day trademark and commercial rights. A certain well-known dripping red wax brand broke new ground while protecting itself against an even better-known tequila giant (and its global spirits owner).[11] And bourbon lawsuits are now defining standards of practice for the entire spirits industry for labeling and truth-in-advertising issues.[12]

Just as there are no shortages of old bourbon lawsuits to tell the story of American history, bourbon remains at the forefront of present-day litigation. Bourbon distillers have always found the right balance between innovation and tradition and mixing Kentucky charm with cutthroat litigation, which makes telling the history of America through the lens of bourbon lawsuits all the more entertaining.

TWO

American Law Defines Bourbon

The question "What is bourbon?" is a bit more complicated than might be anticipated, with thanks again to laws. "What is whiskey?" is a broader question and a little easier to answer. Whiskey is essentially, in its most basic form, a spirit distilled from grain. The type of grain(s) used, the location of distillation, and nature of aging, along with many other factors, then dictate the *type* of whiskey (or whisky), including broad categories such as Scotch, Irish, Canadian, or Japanese and innumerable subcategories.[1]

Whiskey, or *whisky*, as a general term, is defined by law in the United States as "an alcoholic distillate from a fermented mash of grain produced at less than 190° proof in such manner that the distillate possesses the taste, aroma, and characteristics generally attributed to whisky, stored in oak containers (except that corn whisky need not be so stored), and bottled at not less than 80° proof, and also includes mixtures of such distillates for which no specific standards of identity are prescribed."[2]

Bourbon is a type of whiskey, and many distillers remind us that "all bourbon is whiskey, but not all whiskey is bourbon." In order to be bourbon, the whiskey must be made in the United States and must strictly meet these criteria:

- made from fermented mash of not less than 51 percent corn;
- distilled to not more than 80 percent alcohol by volume (ABV) (160 proof);
- stored at no more than 62.5 percent ABV (125 proof);
- stored in charred new oak containers; and

- because it is "whisky," bottled at no less than 40 percent ABV (80 proof).[3]

Importantly, the word *bourbon* cannot be used to describe any whiskey not produced in the United States.[4] Other countries have acknowledged this territorial naming right as well through several agreements, including the North American Free Trade Agreement, the United States–European Union Agreement on Nomenclature of Distilled Spirits, and the United States–Australia Free Trade Agreement, which all recognize bourbon whiskey as a distinct product of the United States.[5]

That does not mean, however, that corporate ownership must be American. Indeed, the major American bourbon distillers represent a global cross section of ownership. The very American-sounding Wild Turkey was owned by the French company Pernod Ricard SA until 2009, when it was acquired by the Italian company Davide Campari Milano S.p.A.[6]

A darling of bourbon enthusiasts over the past decade, Four Roses, has been owned by the Japanese company Kirin Company, Ltd., since the Canadian spirits giant the Seagram Company fell apart. Another Japanese company, Suntory, acquired Beam, Inc., in 2015, creating Beam Suntory, and Takara Shuzo Company owns the Ancient Age brands produced by Sazerac-owned Buffalo Trace. World spirits giant British-based Diageo owns the wildly popular Bulleit brand, along with the legendary Stitzel-Weller Distillery in Louisville, and in March 2017 opened its new distillery in nearby Shelby County, Kentucky. Brown-Forman remains as the only United States–based publicly traded bourbon distiller. Privately held Heaven Hill Brands is America's largest private, family-owned producer of bourbon, and St. Louis–based Luxco, Inc., Lexington, Kentucky–based Alltech, Inc., and New Orleans–based Sazerac, Inc., round out the privately held American-owned major distillers.

While legally strict, the prerequisites to qualify as bourbon do *not* include many "rules" popularly believed to be law. One popular misconception (despite every Kentucky distillery tour guide's correction) is that bourbon must be produced in Kentucky. In fact, bourbon can be produced in any state in the union, even Alaska or Hawaii—it just so happens that thanks to history and due to its perfect conditions, Kentucky is responsible for 95 percent of the nation's bourbon. A large share of the remaining 5 percent is distilled just across the Ohio River border in southeastern Indiana, which shares many of Kentucky's geographic characteristics.

There was a time, however, when bourbon was considered to be a Kentucky-only whiskey, as documented by court cases from the early twentieth century. In *United States v. 50 Barrels of Whisky* evidence was presented that any spirit labeled "Bourbon Whisky" must be distilled "from a fermented mixture of grain, of which Indian corn forms the chief part," and be "distilled in the state of Kentucky."[7] Other courts recognized this early limitation too.[8]

Grain percentages have varied over time and from distiller to distiller. One article in 1905 claimed that bourbon is made from 60 percent corn and 40 percent "small grains": "Bourbon whisky is made from corn, rye and barley malt in the proportion 60 per cent corn and 40 per cent small grains, either 30 per cent rye and 10 per cent malt, or 25 per cent rye and 15 per cent malt."[9] Still today, although the 51 percent corn rule is well-known, there is occasionally some confusion about the use of grains other than corn. Legally, however, the type of secondary grain used—after at least 51 percent corn—does not matter. Court decisions through the mid-twentieth century tended to mention rye and malted barley as secondary grains after at least 51 percent corn and also recognized the required use of new charred oak containers.[10]

True enough, the most-used secondary grain in bourbon is rye. But some of the most popular brands today use wheat as the secondary grain, and distillers sometimes experiment with other secondary grains. Most distillers also use a small percentage of malted barley as part of the mash bill. Bourbon with wheat as the secondary grain is often referred to as "wheated bourbon," but that phrase has no distinct legal definition. Similarly, bourbon using rye as the secondary grain is often referred to as "high-rye" or "low-rye," depending on whether the amount of rye grain exceeds somewhere around 15 percent, but again, there is no distinct legal definition, so today, Sazerac produces so-called high-rye bourbon containing less rye grain than the low-rye recipe used by Four Roses.

Storage in a "charred new oak container" has historically been a *barrel*, but the word used in the law is *container*. If a distiller chose to do so—and could make it watertight—bourbon could be aged in a charred new oak box, bucket, cone, or tetrahedron. Additionally, contrary to popular belief, *American* oak or *white* oak are not required; any type of oak will do under the regulation, but American white oak tends to provide the best seal and flavor (red oak is a popular choice for the rick structure inside aging warehouses because termites typically avoid red oak). The size of the oak container is also left to the discretion of the producer, but the standard in the industry is fifty-three gallons. Many craft distilleries use smaller barrels, and Heaven Hill recently released a special edition bourbon aged for fifteen years in sixty-five-gallon barrels. The keys are *new*, *charred*, and *oak*.

Another false rule is minimum aging. An uncountable number of weekend whiskey fans have proclaimed that bourbon must be aged a minimum of two years (some publications with sloppy authors and editors have helped spread this belief). Regrettably, the Supreme Court of Kentucky recently promoted this myth too.[11] To the contrary, a charred new oak container could be filled with bourbon distillate and stored for any length of time, even just momentarily, and the distillate magically becomes "bourbon." The source of the two-year belief is probably that if bourbon is aged in compliance with its rules for two or more years, it becomes "straight bourbon."[12]

Even the word *age* has legal restrictions—producers can only count the period of time that bourbon is stored in charred new oak containers.[13] A statement of age is not always required on a label either, but many consumers view higher age statements as a sign of quality. Age statements are only required if a bourbon has been aged less than four years. Conversely, any bourbon without an age statement has been aged for at least four years.[14] If an age statement is used (whether involuntarily, because it contains bourbon aged less than four years, or voluntarily, because the label makes a reference to age or maturity for marketing purposes) and the bourbon is a blend of different-aged barrels, a label must state the age of the youngest bourbon in the blend.[15] Producers also have the option of listing the respective ages of each of the barrels used in a blend, on a percentage basis of the final product.[16]

Bourbon rules also get a little more complicated because of what is not referenced in the general definition. For example, straight bourbon and any bottled in bond bourbon (which by definition will already be a straight bourbon) cannot contain coloring, flavoring, or other additives. Regulatory agencies have not always provided clear guidance regarding additives. For example, the Alcohol and Tobacco Tax and Trade Bureau (TTB) is the federal agency charged with promulgating regulations regarding labeling of distilled spirits and other alcoholic beverages, and it also reviews and preapproves distilled spirits labels to ensure compliance with applicable laws. The TTB has interpreted the regulations to prohibit additives in non-straight bourbon, but the actual regulations arguably provide this restriction only for straight whiskies.[17] This disconnect, of course, sometimes leaves consumers wondering whether a bourbon that does not use the word *straight* might contain added artificial flavoring.

It could also lead a well-funded spirits producer to use additives in non-straight bourbon, arguing that a literal reading of the regulations allows it: "(i) such harmless coloring, flavoring, or blending materials as are an essential component part of the particular class or type of distilled spirits to which added, and (ii) harmless coloring, flavoring, or blending materials such as caramel, straight malt or straight rye malt whiskies, fruit juices, sugar, infusion of oak chips when approved by the Administrator, or wine, which are not an essential component part of the particular distilled spirits to which added, but which are customarily employed therein in accordance with established trade usage, if such coloring, flavoring, or blending materials do not total more than 2½ percent by volume of the finished product."[18] However, TTB's interpretation is that the phrase "customarily employed therein in accordance with established trade usage" prohibits the use of additives because, since the late 1800s, bourbon producers fought hard to prohibit additives. So, now it is not "customary" for *any* bourbon to contain coloring or flavoring additives.

This fight to establish customary standards for bourbon in the late 1800s and early 1900s was led by producers of straight whiskey against blenders and rectifiers of what Col. E. H. Taylor Jr. called "imitation whisky." The blenders and rectifiers fought back, claiming that their product was actually purer, and due to its substantially lower price, they captured a majority of the market share.[19]

Purity and the definition of bourbon were addressed by the Pure Food and Drug Act of 1906.[20] In *United States v. 50 Barrels of Whisky*—a case enforcing the Pure Food and Drug Act—the court used whiskey to tackle the far-reaching constitutional issue of federal authority over the transportation of goods in interstate commerce.[21] This case established the applicability of the new federal law to the transportation of spirits between states.

In that case, pursuant to the Pure Food and Drug Act, federal authorities seized fifty barrels of distilled spirits being transported from New Orleans to Baltimore. The court held that those barrels were misbranded as "Bourbon Whisky" because they really contained "a distillate of molasses with a slight infusion of sulphuric acid."[22] While *50 Barrels of Whisky* helped end false branding and labeling, producers and rectifiers of grain distillate continued to use *whisky* and *straight whisky* on their labels.

The question "What is whisky?" was finally answered by President William Howard Taft in 1909, in a declaration known as the "Taft Decision." President Taft had already served as U.S. Sixth Circuit Court of Appeals judge from 1892 to 1900, before his single term as president (1908–12), and later he served as U.S. Supreme Court chief justice (1921–30). While he served on the Sixth Circuit, President Taft gained some bourbon law experience in a case in which he found that James E. Pepper had been buying bourbon from other distilleries for years and had been mislabeling it as his own, all the while guaranteeing to the public that it was distilled by him as genuine and unadulterated Old Pepper.[23] This experience helped guide President Taft sixteen years later when he was called upon, as commander in chief, to clarify the Pure Food and Drug Act by defining "straight," "blended," and "imitation" whiskey in the so-called Taft Decision.[24]

President Taft ruled that both sides could use the word *whisky*, but rectifiers had to call their product "blended whisky."[25] "Straight whisky" was protected for Col. E. H. Taylor Jr. and other distillers who made what we know today as bourbon. President Taft railed against the rectifiers who complained that his ruling would hurt their sales by saying that he "only insists upon the statement of the truth of the label" and it was no problem if "they lose their trade merely from a statement of the fact."[26] President Taft's goal was to inform the public "exactly the kind of whisky they buy and drink. If they desire straight whisky, then they can secure it by purchasing what is branded 'straight whisky.' If they are willing to drink whisky made of neutral spirits, then they can buy it under a brand showing it; and if they are content with a blend of flavors made by the mixture of straight whisky and whisky made of neutral spirits, the brand of the blend upon the package will enable them to buy and drink that which they desire."[27]

The question "What is bourbon?" is very well defined today, but in the American way there are a number of legally defined subcategories and non–legally defined marketing terms. *Bottled in bond* adds an additional set of requirements on top of those already existing for straight bourbon, but *craft* and *small batch* seem to have taken more of a foothold with consumers. The basic question of whether a spirit is bourbon should safely be answered on the label, but consumers should know the meanings of various label phrases.

Not all whiskey is bourbon. Some bottles of brown spirits in the whiskey aisle are not bourbon. Labels that do not contain the word *bourbon* (and more specifically, *straight bourbon*, which should be the goal) are not bourbon. Even looking solely for the word *bourbon* is dangerous because "Whiskey Distilled from Bourbon Mash"

Willett

Bardstown, Kentucky

Pure Kentucky XO, Kentucky Straight Bourbon Whiskey

Age: Unstated

Proof: 107 proof

Cost: $30.00

Notes: A sourced whiskey and part of Willett's Small Batch Boutique lineup, Pure Kentucky XO is an excellent example of an elegant, complex bourbon. Flavors of corn pudding, caramel, coconut, oak, leather, black pepper, and distinct malt round out this sleeper among high-proof brands.

---

is not bourbon. One brand in particular bottles something called "sour mash whiskey" and "American whiskey"; those are not bourbon either. The worst offender may be 2018's Crown Royal Bourbon Mash Blended Canadian Whisky, which gained TTB approval despite the apparent violation of the rule against using the word *bourbon* to describe a whiskey not produced in the United States. Crown Royal withdrew its label after an outcry from bourbon enthusiasts.

Look for straight bourbon. Straight bourbon is bourbon that has been aged a minimum of two years, with no additives other than pure water.[28] The term *straight whiskey* came into existence just before the Civil War to distinguish natural barrel aging from artificially coloring and flavoring by rectifiers.[29]

Look for Kentucky bourbon. If *Kentucky* is in the name, the bourbon must have been produced in Kentucky from grains cooked, fermented, and distilled in Kentucky and aged for "a period of not less than one (1) full year." It can still be removed and aged or bottled elsewhere, but then the name *Kentucky* cannot be used, at the risk of license revocation.[30]

Purity is pure marketing. *Pure* is a term that was more important in the late 1800s and early 1900s than it is today, due to rectifiers, and the courts helped define the term as being "free from extraneous matter; separate from matter of another kind; free from mixture, unmixed."[31] Since the early 1900s, courts held that adding neutral spirits to whiskey could not be called "pure" and that advertising it as pure was "grossly to deceive the public." Some brands, like Pure Kentucky XO, still use the term, which is uncontroversial today.

What's the proof? While bourbon must be bottled at a minimum of 80 proof,[32] there is no maximum proof, and in recent years consumers have demanded bourbon uncut by water, as if it were straight from the barrel. *Barrel strength* (e.g., Four Roses Private Selection Single Barrel), *barrel proof* (e.g., Elijah Craig 12-Year Barrel Proof), and *cask strength* (e.g., Maker's Mark Cask Strength) refer to bourbon that is not diluted with water before bottling. It can range from single barrels (like Four Roses) to large batches (like Wild Turkey Rare Breed).

Four Roses

Lawrenceburg, Kentucky (distillery)
Cox's Creek, Kentucky (warehouses and bottling)

Four Roses Single Barrel Kentucky Straight Bourbon Whiskey

Age: Unstated

Proof: 100 proof

Cost: $30.00–$40.00

Notes: Four Roses uses its O B S V recipe for its standard single barrel bourbon, which, when decoded, means that it uses the highest rye recipe among all Kentucky distillers (60% corn; 35% rye; 5% malted barley) and a proprietary yeast strain that brings delicate fruitiness to the distillate. The high rye and fruitiness is a perfect pair, resulting in a full-bodied bourbon that shines with ripe dark fruits, caramel, vanilla, cocoa, balanced with expressive oak and maple.

Small batch **is almost meaningless.** *Small batch* is an extremely popular phrase, but it is pure marketing, and it means different things for different distillers and bottlers. On the one hand, some bourbon is bottled in ridiculously large batches or even continually dumped into massive tanks, which in many cases results in more flavor continuity. Some distillers or bottlers consider two to five barrels a small batch. Others use fifteen to twenty barrels. Still others use forty barrels or more. The lesson here is that the term *small batch* tells the consumer nothing at all, unless the actual number of barrels is disclosed. One of the more popular brand examples is Elijah Craig Small Batch.

Single barrel **is slightly more meaningful.** *Single barrel* should be obvious, but it is undefined, legally. For example, there is no regulation that would prohibit the mingling of bourbon from separate original barrels into one barrel and then bottled as coming from a "single barrel." Bottle numbering ("bottle ___ of ___") can be extremely helpful here to ensure that the total number of bottles is consistent with expected production given barrel age and evaporation loss. Wild Turkey's Russell's Reserve used the combined term *small batch single barrel* until 2015, causing some confusion because while neither term is legally defined, there is at least consensus that they mean different things. Four Roses Single Barrel is one of the more popular brands and is an excellent example of transparency because its label provides handwritten barrel and warehouse details.

But *craft* is totally meaningless. *Craft* is another undefined term that has become meaningless. To some producers *craft* is meant to signify artisan qualities, small production, and "farm to bottle" old-world techniques. To other producers it can be a marketer's dream to be able to recast a high-volume, mass-produced brand as something not made in a factory. The Distilled Spirits Council (DISCUS), a national trade association for the major distilled spirits producers in the United States, sets a cap of 84,000 cases annually to qualify as a "small distiller," the American Distilling Institute uses a 52,000 annual case cap, and the American Craft Spirits Association uses a whopping 315,000 annual case cap. Even the world's largest producer of bourbon, Beam Suntory, uses *craft* in its Jim Beam Signature Craft series.

The use of the term *finishing* is the latest trend. "Finished in _____ barrels"— examples of which have included port, Pinot Noir, Cabernet Sauvignon, Zinfandel, Cognac, and sherry barrels— has long been used with other whiskies and is now a growing trend with bourbon. There are no regulations to govern finishing; therefore, open questions remain about whether whiskey is proofed down before finishing or whether it is blended with other barrels before finishing, and often there is no information about the provenance of finishing barrels, their prior use, or the length of finishing. Plus, some bourbon purists contend that finishing violates the core requirements for being called "bourbon" in the first place. But TTB has allowed use of the word bourbon so long as a label explains how it was finished. A popular brand example has been limited gift shop releases of Heaven Hill Select Stock, finished in Cognac barrels.

Heaven Hill

Louisville, Kentucky (distillery)

Jefferson and Nelson Counties, Kentucky (warehouses and bottling)

Heaven Hill Select Stock Kentucky Straight Bourbon Whiskey

Age: Varies, often finished in other barrels

Proof: Varies but often barrel proof

Cost: $150.00–$250.00

Notes: Heaven Hill releases gift shop–only bourbon and some private barrels under the Select Stock label. A particularly unique spring 2014 release was aged eight years before finishing for two additional years in Cognac barrels and sold at barrel proof (130.2 proof) for $250.00. The Cognac influence shines in this wheated bourbon, combining to give it sweet dessert qualities, especially when enjoyed with the right amount of water to reduce the alcohol level.

Finally, *handmade* should be ignored. *Handmade* is one of the more interesting marketing terms for bourbon. At one level bourbon cannot be literally handmade because distillation happens in a still, aging happens in barrels, and bottling happens on an automated line. On another level human hands still control the process and the barrels selected for bottling. Perhaps it was this tension that has led to class action lawsuits against, for example, Maker's Mark for using the term *handmade* on its labels. In the end any consumer who believes that *handmade* literally means "made by hand" is insincere, and courts in Florida and California have dismissed the claims asserted against Maker's Mark.[33]

Combine all of these facets, and the complexity of bourbon makes it all the more American. Bourbon has even been called "America's Native Spirit" after Congress declared it to be "a distinctive product of the United States" in 1964:

Bourbon Whiskey Designated as Distinctive Product of U.S.

Whereas "Bourbon whiskey" is a distinctive product of the United States and is unlike other types of alcoholic beverages, whether foreign or domestic; and

Whereas to be entitled to the designation "Bourbon whiskey" the product must conform to the highest standards and must be manufactured in accordance with the laws and regulations of the United States which prescribe a standard of identity for "Bourbon whiskey"; and

Whereas Bourbon whiskey has achieved recognition and acceptance throughout the world as a distinctive product of the United States:

Now, therefore, be it

Resolved by the Senate (the House of Representatives concurring),

That it is the sense of Congress that the recognition of Bourbon whiskey as a distinctive product of the United States be brought to the attention of the appropriate agencies of the United States Government toward the end that such agencies will take appropriate action to prohibit the importation into the United States of whisky designated as "Bourbon whiskey."[34]

Bourbon is unique, but America has always had its share of imitators. Bourbon takes time and patience to mature, but it is the American way to innovate and cut production time. Bourbon is strictly defined, but Americans always find ways to test boundaries and argue about the details. That's bourbon.

THREE

Bourbon Drives the Development of Trademark and Brand Name Rights

B ourbon's imprint on commercial rights begins with the origin of a phrase uttered every day around the world: *brand name*. Many people want to wear only "brand-name clothes," while generic or store brand clothes are considered inferior. Companies spend billions of dollars to develop and promote their "brand identity." *Forbes* reported that Lego was named the most powerful brand name in the world in 2017, and we all recognize brands such as Google, Nike, Apple, and Coca-Cola. We also have certain expectations of high quality with these famous brands, and we use them to distinguish companies and products from their rivals.

But how did a product or company name come to be known as a brand? Bourbon has the answer. Beginning in the 1800s, federal law required that "the name of the distiller shall be stamped or burned upon the head of every package of distilled spirits put into bonded warehouses, and this must not be erased until the package is empty."[1] The phrase *brand name* was born from this federal law and the branding of barrels by distillers, and then it spread to other manufactured goods.

Because whiskey was often sold by the barrel, the brand on the barrelhead was important. (Selling by the barrel created its own problems, like refilling with lesser-quality bourbon or blending with lesser-quality bourbon or watering it down to make it last longer. Those issues were addressed by the innovation of bottling with signed seals over the closure.) A barrel branded with *Old Crow* could be sold for a higher price, whether sold in bulk or upon resale. So, just as brand names today are highly sought after and protected, early distillers fought hard to protect their brand names.

Bourbon litigation helped define the parameters of brand name protection, including by limiting the use of one's own family name. The Labrot & Graham Distillery is what Brown-Forman called its distillery in Woodford County, Kentucky, when it began producing Woodford Reserve, although it has since renamed the distillery the Woodford Reserve Distillery. The original name of the distillery, however, plowed new ground for brand name rights.

In October 1880 the grandson of the original owner of the earliest distillery on the Woodford Reserve property sued a partnership of French wine producer Leopold Labrot and Kentucky businessman James H. Graham. The ruling from this lawsuit provides an invaluable outline of some of the earliest distilling operations in Kentucky and the perfection of the bourbon distilling process by James Crow.

According to Brown-Forman's National Historic Landmark Application for the Labrot & Graham's Old Oscar Pepper Distillery, it described the property as a "bourbon whiskey manufacturing complex in Woodford County, Kentucky, standing on a site that has been used for the conversion of grain into alcohol since 1812, when Elijah Pepper, a farmer-distiller, established his 350 acre farm."[2]

Elijah Pepper, a Virginian who moved to Kentucky in 1797, established his first distillery behind the Woodford County Courthouse in Versailles around 1810.[3] By 1812, however, Elijah Pepper had acquired hundreds of acres along Glenn's Creek, where he built his homestead, a gristmill, and a distillery and where he established his family farm.[4] Elijah Pepper died in early 1831, and the distillery was then operated by his son, Oscar N. Pepper.[5] After Oscar completed a new limestone distillery building in 1838, the distillery became known as the "Old Oscar Pepper Distillery."[6] By 1833, and through 1855 (except for two years), Oscar Pepper employed the venerable James Crow as his distiller, and the distillery was renowned for its bourbon and for refining and defining what we know as bourbon today.[7]

James Crow died in April 1856, but because of the fame gained by the Crow brand, Old Crow bourbon continued to be produced at the Old Oscar Pepper distillery by W. F. Mitchell, who had worked with and then succeeded James Crow as distiller.[8] Oscar Pepper died in June 1865, and it appears that the property containing the distillery was transferred by the estate to Oscar's youngest of seven children, O'Bannon Pepper.[9] O'Bannon was still a minor, which meant that Oscar's wife, Nannie, controlled the distillery. She leased the distillery property in 1870 to Gaines, Berry & Company of Frankfort, although James E. Pepper—Oscar's eldest son—may have managed the distillery.[10] Gaines, Berry & Company produced "Old Crow Whiskey," called the distillery the "Old Crow Distillery," and continued to employ W. F. Mitchell as their distiller.[11]

James Pepper sued his mother in 1872 to gain control of the distillery property, and after succeeding in taking control of the distillery, he then partnered with Col. E. H. Taylor Jr., who had parted ways with Gaines, Berry & Company, to make improvements to the distillery and continue operations.[12] The case of *Pepper v. Labrot* picks up where the National Historical Landmark Application leaves off.[13] In 1874 Gaines, Berry & Company took the Old Crow trademark along to another of its distillery operations, leaving James Pepper with the Old Oscar Pepper brand, also known as O.O.P. "bourbon."[14]

James Pepper experienced financial hardships and was declared bankrupt in 1877.[15] Through the bankruptcy Colonel Taylor took sole ownership of the Old Oscar Pepper Distillery.[16] But Colonel Taylor—who owned many other distilleries—experienced his own financial ruin shortly thereafter, even having to leave Kentucky to avoid his creditors.[17] This led to the transfer of the Old Oscar Pepper Distillery to George T. Stagg.[18] In 1878 it was sold to Labrot & Graham.[19]

James Pepper's financial fortunes seemed to have reversed, and he built a new distillery on Old Frankfort Pike in Lexington, Kentucky.[20] There he hoped to continue to trade on his father's name and the tremendous reputation achieved by his father and James Crow.[21] The problem was that Labrot & Graham was using the Old Oscar Pepper brand and was still calling the distillery the "Old Oscar Pepper Distillery."[22] James believed that only he should be able to

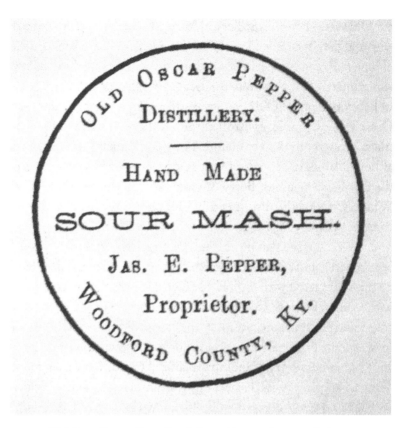

FIG. 1. Old Oscar Pepper Barrelhead–James Pepper. *Pepper v. Labrot*, 1881.

use the Pepper name, and in 1880 he filed a lawsuit in federal court to gain back part of what he had lost in bankruptcy.[23]

After reciting the history of the property and the claims and counterclaims being asserted, the court noted and relied upon an advertisement used by James Pepper from the period when he owned the Old Oscar Pepper Distillery. James credited his bourbon's quality to his father's distillery and the terroir: "Having put in the most thorough running order the old distillery premises of my father, the late Oscar Pepper (now owned by me), I offer to the first-class trade of this country a hand-made, sour-mash, pure copper whisky of perfect excellence. The celebrity attained by the whisky made by my father was ascribable to the excellent water used (a very superior spring), and the grain grown on the farm adjoining by himself, and to the process observed by James Crow, after his death by William F. Mitchell, his distillers. I am now running the distillery with the same distiller, the same water, the same formulas, and grain grown upon the same farm."[24]

Despite Oscar Pepper's much earlier ownership of the distillery, James alleged that the name Old Oscar Pepper had not been used until 1874.[25] He claimed that the brand that he burned on barrel-heads was his trademark (fig. 1).[26]

As might be expected, evidence was presented to the court proving that between 1838 and 1865, while Oscar Pepper operated the distillery, it was already commonly known as the "Oscar Pepper Distillery."[27] Additionally, because of the fame of James Crow and his bourbon—known as "Old Crow"—the distillery was also known as the "Old Crow Distillery," a name that continued in use after James Crow died in 1856 and after Oscar Pepper died in 1865.[28] Even Gaines, Berry & Company marketed themselves as "Lessees of Oscar Pepper's 'Old Crow' Distillery."[29]

After James Pepper lost the property and after the eventual acquisition by Labrot & Graham, Labrot & Graham used a similar brand for its barrel-heads and specifically used the name Old Oscar Pepper Distillery (fig. 2).[30] Labrot & Graham responded to the lawsuit by explaining that it was using the name Old Oscar Pepper Distillery properly because the distillery it now owned was called the "Old Oscar Pepper Distillery."[31] The court posed two questions: should Labrot & Graham be forced to change the name of a distillery that it purchased and denied the right to call the distillery by its name, and, conversely, should James Pepper be allowed to continue to use the name of his father's former distillery, when his new bourbon was not distilled there?[32]

As might be expected by the way the court presented these questions, Labrot & Graham won the case.[33] The court ruled that reference to *Old Oscar Pepper's Distillery* meant the place of production and was not a trademark.[34] Moreover, James could not

FIG. 2. Old Oscar Pepper Barrelhead–Labrot & Graham.
Pepper v. Labrot, 1881.

truthfully use the phrase since he no longer owned the Old Oscar Pepper Distillery.[35]

While Col. E. H. Taylor Jr. was only tangentially involved in *Pepper v. Labrot*, he made his mark on bourbon law through several of his own cases. In fact, a series of cases from the late 1800s and early 1900s helped establish the boundaries for trademark protection in a name, as illustrated through Colonel Taylor's fanciful script signature (a trademark still used today).

Colonel Taylor acquired his first distillery on the banks of the Kentucky River in 1869, on property that is now known as "Buffalo Trace." Colonel Taylor christened his distillery the "O.F.C." (Old Fire Copper or Old Fashioned Copper) Distillery, and there

FIG. 3. Edmund H. Taylor Jr. script signature. *Geo T. Stagg Co. v. Taylor*, 1894.

he produced the famous O.F.C. whiskey brand. While *O.F.C.* was the focus, Colonel Taylor adopted a script signature as part of his branding (fig. 3).

As described in *Newcomb-Buchanan Co. v. Baskett*, Colonel Taylor's troubles were brewing at least by the spring of 1875.[36] Just months before the running of the first Kentucky Derby, Taylor sold 150 barrels to J. S. Baskett, a Henry County farmer who raised Hereford cattle and was a banker—both passions he shared with Colonel Taylor.[37] Baskett paid for the bourbon and paid the taxes, so the barrels were to be moved from the bonded warehouse at the O.F.C. to a free warehouse (fig. 4).[38]

Instead of honoring his sale to Baskett, Colonel Taylor *sold the same 150 barrels* to Newcomb-Buchanan Company (one of the largest distillery groups in Kentucky at the time) to cover debts Colonel Taylor owed.[39] Newcomb-Buchanan, in turn, sold 25 of Baskett's barrels and credited Taylor's account, shipped another 101 of Baskett's barrels to George T. Stagg in St. Louis to cover debt Colonel Taylor owed to Stagg, and still had the remaining

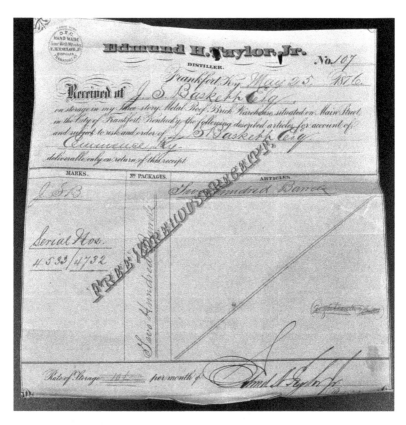

FIG. 4. Free warehouse receipt from E. H. Taylor Jr. to J. S. Baskett. *Newcomb-Buchanan Co. v. Baskett*, Oldham Circuit Court, 1879. Kentucky State Archives.

barrels when Baskett came looking for his bourbon during the summer of 1877.[40]

Colonel Taylor was nowhere to be found. In the Buffalo Trace Oral History Project, Colonel Taylor's great-great-grandson says that Colonel Taylor fled to Europe and left one of his sons behind to deal with the creditors, but the court simply noted that "in May, 1877, Taylor left the state on account of pecuniary troubles," so Baskett sued Newcomb-Buchanan.[41] The Oldham Circuit Court record shows another reason that Colonel Taylor might have disappeared: the court had issued an arrest warrant against him, as requested by Newcomb-Buchanan.[42]

Buffalo Trace

Frankfort, Kentucky

E. H. Taylor Small Batch Bottled in Bond Kentucky Straight Bourbon Whiskey

Age: Unstated

Proof: 100 proof

Cost: $50.00

Notes: Sazerac bought the Old Taylor brand from Beam and moved it to the property he briefly oversaw, back when it was known as the "O.F.C. Distillery." In reality, though, Colonel Taylor solidified his legendary status at a different distillery, the property in Millville, Kentucky, still known today as the "Old Taylor Distillery" and which is producing bourbon again under new ownership and the Castle & Key brand name. Regardless, this bottled in bond variety is a classic, robust bourbon, with highlights of brown sugar, caramel, clove, and tobacco. It's earthy—almost on the verge of musty—but a solid bourbon all the same.

Newcomb-Buchanan defended on the ground that it simply did not know about Baskett's ownership of the barrels. The court of appeals ruled in favor of Baskett, reasoning that Newcomb-Buchanan never had an ownership interest in the barrels because Colonel Taylor never had the right to (re)sell the barrels in the first place, and instructed the trial court to assess damages in favor of Baskett.[43] Colonel Taylor's debt went far beyond what might be saved by a double sale, however. He needed a buyout, and he needed it fast.

In December 1877 George T. Stagg, a St. Louis whiskey merchant and a large creditor of Colonel Taylor, bought Colonel Taylor out of bankruptcy by paying twenty cents on the dollar to the creditors.[44] In exchange Stagg became the owner of the O.F.C. Distillery and the O.F.C. trademark.[45] Stagg leased the O.F.C. back to Colonel Taylor, and, the court noted, O.F.C. whiskey "attain[ed] a phenomenal reputation."[46] A year later the success of Colonel Taylor and Stagg allowed them to build the Carlisle Distillery next to O.F.C., and they continued to enjoy great success.[47]

Stagg took measures to protect the O.F.C. trade name and the business. He formed the E. H. Taylor, Jr. Company in 1879 and registered the O.F.C. trademark.[48] Stagg was the president and majority shareholder of the company, and Colonel Taylor was the vice president, apparently owning just a single share.[49] Importantly, the trademark registrations focused on *O.F.C.* and not on the use of Colonel Taylor's name.[50] In time, however, the use of Colonel Taylor's name became more and more prominent, finally resulting in the use, in 1880, of the well-known script signature.[51]

The court summarized the evolution of using Colonel Taylor's script signature on O.F.C. whiskey. Colonel Taylor (and Stagg) began by simply noting Colonel Taylor's name, as the distiller, in normal font under the O.F.C. brand name.[52] By 1881 they used what the court characterized as "the well-known and striking autograph signature of E. H. Taylor, Jr.," using the signature to "prove" that the whiskey was genuine O.F.C. whiskey.[53] But this script signature was never protected by Stagg as a trademark.[54]

Stagg and Colonel Taylor parted ways toward the end of 1886, and effective January 1, 1887, the split was official.[55] Stagg retained the O.F.C. and Carlisle Distilleries, and Colonel Taylor acquired for himself the J. S. Taylor Distillery in Millville, Woodford County, Kentucky, which had been owned and operated by one of Colonel Taylor's sons before becoming part of Stagg's E. H. Taylor, Jr. Company in 1882.[56]

Colonel Taylor immediately formed a partnership with his sons, J. Swigert and Kenner, again using his name for the name of the business: E. H. Taylor, Jr. & Sons.[57] He renamed the distillery the "Old Taylor Distillery" and immediately started using the same script signature that he had previously used with his O.F.C. bourbon, except he added *& Sons*.[58] *This* is the distillery—not the O.F.C.—where Colonel Taylor solidified his legendary position in Kentucky bourbon lore. He built a castle, pioneered a new mar-

FIG. 5. Old Taylor Bottled in Bond label. *E. H. Taylor Jr. & Sons v. Geo. T. Stagg Co.*, Franklin Circuit Court, March 9, 1898. Kentucky State Archives.

riage between production and aesthetics, and created his namesake iconic brand (fig. 5).

In the meantime Stagg, who formed the George T. Stagg Company after his split with Colonel Taylor, was in the process of making improvements to the O.F.C. and Carlisle Distilleries, which remained idle for eighteen months.[59] The court had no doubt that Stagg's "ambitious purpose" was "to substitute his own name, or that of the corporation bearing his name, as the distiller and proprietor of the famous O.F.C. and Carlisle Distilleries."[60] However, when Stagg resumed production in January 1889, he started using Colonel Taylor's script signature instead.[61]

Buffalo Trace

Frankfort, Kentucky

Stagg Jr. Kentucky Straight Bourbon Whiskey

Age: Unstated

Proof: Varies with batch (usually above 130 proof)

Cost: $55.00–$65.00

Notes: Taking its name from George T. Stagg—who bought Colonel Taylor out of bankruptcy and took over ownership of the O.F.C.—Stagg Jr. also harks back to the highly acclaimed Buffalo Trace Antique Collection George T. Stagg bourbon, but as *Jr.* indicates, it is not quite as old. Still, Stagg Jr. is an unfiltered, barrel-strength powerhouse. Sometimes too hot, Stagg Jr. will never be considered a "sweet" bourbon.

So, Colonel Taylor sued Stagg on October 16, 1889, asking for an injunction to stop Stagg from using the company name of E. H. Taylor, Jr. Company or his script signature and for monetary damages.[62] The Franklin circuit court, in Frankfort, Kentucky, noted in its 1891 judgment that Colonel Taylor had named his distillery the "O.F.C." but that the trademarks consisted only of the O.F.C. and Carlisle names; Colonel Taylor's script signature used on the free end of barrels and on labels was not part of the trademark.[63] This ruling gave Colonel Taylor the exclusive right to use his name and script signature, and the trial court ruled that it was "untruthful" for Stagg to use Colonel Taylor's name in any way for whiskey made after January 1, 1887.[64] After an appeal by Stagg, in 1894 the Kentucky Court of Appeals agreed and sided with Colonel Taylor, prohibiting Stagg from using the script signature on any bourbon distilled after January 1, 1887 (because Colonel Taylor *was* the distiller before that date).[65]

In answering the question of whether the script signature became a trademark owned by Stagg, the court of appeals looked into the origin of the script signature and noted the testimony of Colonel

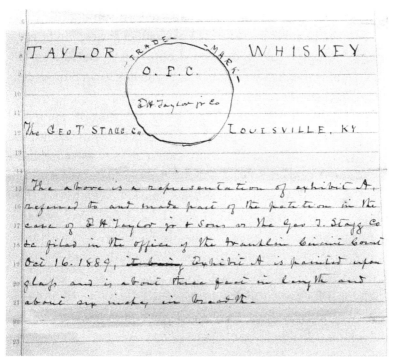

FIG. 6. O.F.C. trademark registration transferred from Colonel Taylor to Stagg, which emphasized "O.F.C." as the essential feature. *E. H. Taylor Jr. & Sons v. Geo. T. Stagg Co.*, Kentucky State Archives.

Taylor and Stagg: "Stagg says that on one occasion, when Taylor was in St. Louis, the latter noticed a striking script signature on packages of imported brandy, and was impressed with the idea that the signature of the company, as written by him, would be appropriate, and look well on a barrel. Taylor suggested it. Stagg agreed with him, and it was done. . . . Taylor contends that it was a mere fancy with him, and was intended to show his personal identification with the distilling operations of the company."[66]

The court of appeals then analyzed the actual trademark registration and transfer from Colonel Taylor to Stagg, which emphasized *O.F.C.* as the essential feature, as shown in a handwritten exhibit from the trial (fig. 6).[67]

The name of Colonel Taylor, the court held, merely identified him as the distiller, and the court expected any subsequent distiller's name to be substituted for that of Colonel Taylor.[68] In fact, the court of appeals recognized that any continued use of Colonel Taylor's name as the distiller—after a time when he ceased to actually be the distiller—would have been improper.[69]

But just like the Franklin circuit court, the court of appeals did not award any monetary damages, and Colonel Taylor was not satisfied with just an injunction.[70] He wanted money, so he asked the court to reconsider its decision about damages.[71] In 1896 the Kentucky Court of Appeals rejected the damages claim for a second time, and maybe in an effort to quiet Colonel Taylor's complaints, the court noted that its 1894 ruling in his favor "was with some reluctance."[72] Nevertheless, the court of appeals asked the lower court to examine the issue of damages again.[73]

Colonel Taylor remained persistent, and he continued to push the issue of damages with the Franklin Circuit Court, where he won on the issue and was finally awarded monetary damages.[74] Showing the same resolve as Colonel Taylor, the Geo. T. Stagg Company appealed to the Kentucky Court of Appeals.[75] Finally, in 1902—after nearly thirteen years of litigation—Colonel Taylor lost the damages issue for good.[76] His loss might have been predictable, given the court's 1894 brushback, but this litigation story shows that persistence was certainly one of Colonel Taylor's character traits.

Persistence, of course, remains an American trait too, and persistence was needed over one hundred years later by Maker's Mark to fight back against a popular tequila brand and the world's largest spirits company, over one of bourbon's most recognizable trademarks— the dripping red wax of Maker's Mark. Ever since Maker's Mark began production in 1958, after Bill Samuels Sr. broke from Country Distillers and struck out on his own, Maker's Mark has capped its bottles with a red wax seal that partially covers the neck of the bottle and drips down to the bottle's shoulder. As noted by the district court in *Maker's Mark Distillery, Inc. v. Diageo North America, Inc.*, "That design was the brainchild of Margie Samuels, mother of Maker's Mark's current president Bill Samuels, who was still at home when his mother perfected the dripping wax in their family's basement."[77]

Maker's Mark registered this trademark in 1985, describing it as the "wax-like coating covering the cap of the bottle and trickling down the neck of the bottle in a freeform irregular pattern."[78] This move coincided with an extensive marketing push by Maker's Mark, and through even more marketing ($22 million annually in 2010), the company eventually reversed its ratio of selling 90 percent of its bourbon in Kentucky to selling 90 percent of its bourbon outside of Kentucky (fig. 7).[79]

Problems arose in 2001, when Diageo—the world's largest spirits company—marketed Jose Cuervo Reserva de La Familia, which used a red free-form waxlike seal cap.[80] After Maker's Mark filed its complaint in 2003, Jose Cuervo started snipping the wax tendrils on the Reserva de La Familia bottles, although it continued to use a red wax seal. Diageo also used the lawsuit to go on the offensive, asking the court to cancel Maker's Mark's trademark on the ground that it was functional and because other alcoholic beverages were already being sealed in colorful wax.[81] A six-week trial was held beginning in November 2009.[82] Bill Samuels testified, along with Master Distiller Kevin Smith, company finance and marketing officers, and even experts on issues such as spirits markets and consumer recognition of brands, damages, wax composition, Maker's Mark memorabilia, and bottle closures.[83]

On April 2, 2010, the district court ruled that Diageo had infringed on Maker's Mark's trademark, and therefore it issued an injunction in favor of Maker's Mark.[84] But the court refused to award any monetary damages because Maker's Mark did not prove that anyone had *actually* been confused or that it had lost any sales, although the court still awarded nearly $67,000 to Maker's Mark to offset its attorneys' fees and expenses of bringing the lawsuit.

The case was far from over, however. Diageo appealed to the United States Court of Appeals for the Sixth Circuit.[85] On appeal Diageo argued that purchasers of Jose Cuervo Reserva de la Familia—"a $100 per bottle luxury tequila"—were unlikely to ever be

FIG. 7. Maker's Mark iconic red dripping wax trade dress. Author's collection.

confused that their prized tequila was affiliated with an inexpensive bourbon like Maker's Mark, especially Cuervo consumers, who "generally are tequila connoisseurs who spend more than $100 for a bottle of tequila, or $16–20 for a drink in a bar."[86]

Plus, Diageo argued, Maker's Mark was hardly the first company to use a dripping wax seal on a bottle.[87] Wax seals have been used for centuries, and Diageo emphasized that Bill Samuels admitted that the inspiration for the Maker's Mark free-form wax coating was old Cognac bottles with wax seals and an irregular or uneven edge.[88] Maker's Mark's experts admitted that numerous other bourbons and other spirits have used red wax seals or dripping wax seals.[89] Wines and even beers have also used wax seals, many of them red and many with tendrils.[90] Nonalcoholic products such as olive oil and vinegar have also used red dripping wax seals.[91] So, why should Maker's Mark get special protection?

The answer to that question became evident by reading only the opening lines of the Sixth Circuit's May 9, 2012, ruling, emphasizing that while bourbon has distinct economic force, it also is entitled to protect its assets in the courts: "Justice Hugo Black once wrote, 'I was brought up to believe that Scotch whisky would need a tax preference to survive in competition with Kentucky bourbon.' *Dep't of Revenue v. James B. Beam Distilling Co.*, 377 U.S. 341, 348–49 [1964] (Black, J., dissenting). While there may be some truth to Justice Black's statement that paints Kentucky bourbon as such an economic force that its competitors need government protection or preference to compete with it, it does not mean a Kentucky bourbon distiller may not also avail itself of our laws to protect its assets."[92]

The outcome became even clearer when the court gave a veritable history lesson about bourbon, discussing:

- the origin and history of bourbon;
- the difference between "whiskey" and "bourbon";
- the different spellings of *whiskey* and *whisky*;
- bourbon mash bills and Dr. James Crow's perfection of the sour mash method;

- early marketing of bourbon and early fans, like Ulysses S. Grant and Henry Clay;
- the rise and fall of rectifiers and President William Taft's 1909 interpretation of the 1906 Pure Food and Drug Act;
- distiller consolidation after the repeal of National Prohibition;
- more name-dropping of bourbon fans, like President Harry S. Truman and Ian Fleming, who reportedly switched from martinis to bourbon;
- the action of Congress, in 1964, to designate bourbon as a "'distinctive product of the United States,' 27 C.F.R. § 5.22(*l*)(1), and prescribed restrictions on which distilled spirits may bear the label 'bourbon'";
- the Samuels family's important role in the history of bourbon ("Maker's Mark occupies a central place in the modern story of bourbon"), including having been distillers since the 1783; and
- Maker's Mark's rise, especially after the now legendary 1980 *Wall Street Journal* front-page article about Maker's Mark, and craft bourbon generally, that garnered national attention for the bourbon, the red dripping wax seal, and the family behind it.[93]

Despite spending four pages on this significant history, the circuit court did not discuss any of the even longer history of tequila (dating back to the sixteenth century) or Jose Antonio de Cuervo's purchase of a blue agave farm from King Ferdinand VI of Spain in 1758 and instead wrote a mere three sentences, only to reference the name of the Cuervo brand, its initial use of a straight-edged wax seal, and its transition in 2001 to a "red dripping wax seal reminiscent of the Maker's Mark red dripping wax seal."[94] Then the circuit court went on to affirm the injunction and the award of litigation expenses to Maker's Mark, protecting Maker's Mark's exclusive use of its red dripping wax seal.[95]

Many other bourbon brands use wax seals today, but none use red, and all are neatly trimmed. No brand seems willing to use red wax at all or free-form tendrils of any color. That seemed to be part of the district court's reasoning for imposing an injunction: the court recognized that its ruling "also protects Maker's Mark from other competitors or quasi-competitors in the industry, in that it may serve to discourage them from treading too closely on the mark."[96]

TASTING NOTES

Maker's Mark
Loretto, Kentucky

Maker's Mark Kentucky Straight Bourbon Whisky

Age: Unstated

Proof: 90 proof

Cost: $30.00–$35.00

Notes: Maker's Mark is flavor-forward bourbon (sweet) that is remarkably clean and crisp and actually mouthwatering. Maker's Mark is one of the few bourbons that uses wheat (instead of rye) as the secondary grain and is barreled at the comparatively low 110 proof. Maker's Mark is also the only major distillery that rotates its barrels to create more consistency among them. The barrels begin their aging on the top three warehouse floors for the first three summers, then they are rotated down, which evens out the taste profile, along with using a formula for pulling barrels for batches from different warehouses, providing even more consistency.

Maker's Mark Cask Strength Kentucky Straight Bourbon Whisky

Age: Unstated

Proof: Usually around 110 proof (varies depending on batch)

Cost: $38.00 (375 mL)

Notes: In a case of management accepting consumer and bartender demands, Marker's Mark finally released a cask-strength version of its standard bourbon (and, later, of Maker's Mark 46). Due to the ability to compare Maker's Mark Cask Strength with the standard-proofed option, this offering shows the benefits of cask strength—an intensification of aromas and flavors, in particular creamy vanilla, caramel, raisins, honey, and oak, with a long, warming finish. Bartenders like it for its higher proof, but this is a great bourbon for sipping neat.

Maker's Mark 46 Kentucky Straight Bourbon Whisky

Age: Unstated

Proof: 94 proof

Cost: $32.00–$40.00

Notes: Maker's Mark 46 (introduced in 2010) begins with fully matured Maker's Mark, which is emptied from the barrel. Then ten seared eighteen-month-old French oak staves are inserted into the barrel, and the same bourbon is returned to that barrel and aged for another eight to eleven weeks. This process provides a bolder bourbon without the tannins, with richer sweetness of butterscotch, cherry, and chocolate and a longer, lingering finish. A cask-strength version was added in 2015, and in 2016 Maker's Mark began a private barrel program in which participants can select among a variety of different finishing staves for a personalized bourbon.

FOUR

Old Crow Provides the Most Comprehensive
Trade Name Case Study

Bourbon distillers have proven themselves to be a competitive bunch, and taking advantage of another's name recognition is probably as old as commercial distilling itself. Col. E. H. Taylor Jr., George T. Stagg, James E. Pepper, Country Distillers, Maker's Mark, and countless others have all sued to protect their trade names or trademarks. One brand rises above the rest, however, both in sheer number of lawsuits and in telling the American story: Old Crow.

The Old Crow brand is named after Dr. James Crow, the Scottish immigrant who many claim invented or perfected the sour mash method of distilling bourbon at the Old Oscar Pepper Distillery (now Woodford Reserve). From the 1830s through his death in 1855, the Old Oscar Pepper Distillery was renowned for Dr. Crow's bourbon, which became known as "Old Crow." Old Crow continued in production after 1855 by W. F. Mitchell (who had worked with and then succeeded Dr. Crow as distiller) and beyond. Solomon C. Herbst, the Prussian-born wholesaler who bought the Old Judge Distillery and is the origin of the John E. Fitzgerald legend, testified that Old Crow was the best and most expensive whiskey.[1]

Old Crow is perhaps the most celebrated historical brand, but in more recent decades it has transitioned to the bottom shelf.[2] While the stories about Dr. Crow have largely morphed into marketing legends, numerous cases from the late 1800s and early 1900s preserve the true story of the brand, shine light on the corporate appropriation of an abandoned brand name, and show that litigiousness is an old American trait.

More than a decade after Dr. Crow died, Gaines, Berry & Company was formed as a partnership by Hiram Berry, William A. Gaines, and Col. E. H. Taylor Jr. Later it was reconstituted as W. A. Gaines & Company when it added New York investors and management Sherman Paris, Marshall J. Allen, and Frank S. Stevens. They built the Hermitage Distillery in Frankfort, Kentucky, in 1868, and reportedly became the largest producer of sour mash whiskies in the world. Colonel Taylor withdrew in 1870 to pursue his own distillery ambitions, and new New York money and management continued to be added.

As might be expected, the Civil War had curtailed whiskey production dramatically. But after the end of the war production across Kentucky ramped up quickly and producers began using more sophisticated and scientific methods, such as those used by Dr. Crow before the war. The Old Crow brand had received some notoriety during the war, and Colonel Taylor and his partners saw an opportunity with the death of Oscar Pepper. Gaines, Berry & Company leased the Old Oscar Pepper Distillery and employed Dr. Crow's apprentice, and the company immediately began branding its barrel-heads "Old Crow." Upon the expiration of its lease, the company moved to a new distillery a few miles down Glenn's Creek toward Frankfort, naming it the "Old Crow Distillery."

Eleven published court opinions between 1898 and 1918 tell the story of Dr. Crow, the Old Oscar Pepper Distillery, the new Old Crow Distillery, and the ongoing efforts of Gaines, Berry & Company to protect the brand name that it had acquired. In addition to the factual historical value of these cases, they also show the fierce tenacity that today is more commonplace in brand name protection. In fact, as marketing hit its modern stride in the 1950s, Old Crow took great pride in its history of lawsuits and wore courtroom battles as a badge of pride (fig. 8).[3]

To set the stage, the Old Oscar Pepper Distillery is situated on Glenn's Creek in Woodford County, Kentucky. Only a few miles downstream toward the Kentucky River and Frankfort are the famous Old Taylor Distillery and the Old Crow Distillery. This stretch of

FIG. 8. Old Crow 1954 advertisement. *LIFE*, September 15, 1952. Author's collection.

Glenn's Creek might be one of the "sweet spots" for bourbon production, as noted by the United States Court of Appeals for the Sixth Circuit in 1915: "Woodford County, Ky., is not far from Bourbon County, and is in the heart of the limestone formation, 'blue grass' country. This general region has always been and is the center of the distilling business for the best known Kentucky whiskies.

The water from the limestone springs—whether or not it is really better than other waters for making whisky—in the early days was thought to be of unique purity and essential to the highest grade of the distilled product. Three brands, among the most advertised and so most widely known now for a generation, are made within a few miles of each other, in Woodford County, along Glenn's creek— 'Taylor,' 'Pepper,' and 'Crow.'"[4]

The cases then describe how Dr. Crow "had a secret formula for the making of whisky" and "was employed in 1833 by Oscar Pepper, the owner and operator of a distillery, for whom he made whisky according to his formula until 1855."[5] After Dr. Crow died, his apprentice, William F. Mitchell, "who had worked with Crow and had learned his formula, took Crow's place and continued to make whisky at the Pepper distillery" until 1865, when Oscar Pepper died.[6] Gaines, Berry & Company leased the Pepper Distillery after Pepper died, until July 1869, at which time Gaines, Berry & Company moved to a new distillery about three miles away down Glenn's Creek.[7] Gaines, Berry & Company (and its successor, W. A. Gaines & Co.) employed Mitchell as its distiller both while leasing the Oscar Pepper Distillery and at its new distillery, all the while using Dr. Crow's secret formula.[8] In order to ensure the link to Dr. Crow and his secret formula, Gaines hired Mitchell's apprentice, Van Johnson, who learned the secret formula from Mitchell, as its distiller in 1872.[9] Gaines, therefore, was able to tie its use of the Old Crow formula and the Old Crow name directly back to Dr. Crow himself.

The Old Crow brand—whether distilled by Crow, Mitchell, or Johnson—was highly regarded as "a whisky of superior excellence and quality" and was "sold at a higher price than any other whisky of equal age produced in the United States."[10] Despite having first used the Old Crow name in 1867, for some unknown reason Gaines claimed in an 1882 trademark application that his company had used the name continuously only since January 1870, when it built the Old Crow Distillery.[11] Then, in June 1904, Gaines tried to back-date its usage when the company filed another trademark application asserting that the Old Crow trademark "has been continuously used by the said W. A. Gaines & Company and its predecessors since the year AD 1835."[12] Gaines filed yet another trademark registration in 1909 for Old Crow—but this time specifying that the name applied only to "straight bourbon and rye whisky."[13]

The lawsuits all dealt with perceived or actual efforts by others to profit from using the name Old Crow, or arguably similar names, often for rectified whiskey. Gaines initially won its lawsuits, but then, as happens so often with American stories of hubris, Gaines overreached and started losing cases, setting up a decisive final battle.

In the earliest case, in 1898, Gaines won a trademark case in New York against a brand using the name White Crow.[14] Four years later Gaines won another lawsuit against a grocer that had bottled Old Crow as an authorized retailer but who then started using the Crow name for bottling other whiskey.[15] This case helped refine public policy that "the public had the right to presume that the bottles on which defendant had placed the 'Old Crow' labels contained whisky of plaintiff's production," perhaps being a forebear of the Pure Food and Drug Act that would be passed two years later.[16] More specifically, this bourbon lawsuit established ground rules for competition: "Rival manufacturers may lawfully compete for the patronage of the public in the quality and price of their goods, in the beauty and tastefulness of their inclosing packages, in the extent of their advertisements, and in the employment of agents; but they have no right by imitative devices to beguile the public into buying their wares under the impression they are buying those of their rivals."[17]

After these important victories, however, Gaines lost cases when it made tenuous claims of trademark infringement against brands like Raven Valley and Old Jay. These bourbon lawsuits helped put important limits on trademark rights; just because Gaines had rights in Old Crow did not mean that it could stifle legitimate competition or prevent other producers from using a bird name or image.[18] *Raven Valley* and *Old Jay*, although referring to birds, were not close enough to *Old Crow* to cause any confusion, so Gaines lost those cases.

Next, in a series of six cases spanning the period between 1904 and 1918, Gaines took aim at I. & L. M. Hellman Company, a St. Louis rectifier that used the brand name Old Crow along with other versions of the Crow name. To make the obvious trademark implications even more interesting, Hellman was a rectifier that concocted blended whiskey, thus pitting the two arch enemies against each other: a genuine straight whiskey producer against a rectifier.

Each side claimed that its own whiskey was pure and that the other side practically produced deadly poison. For its part Gaines alleged that Hellman "sold a spurious compounded liquor" and complained that Hellman was "fraudulent[ly] . . . imposing upon the public a blended whisky, impure and deleterious."[19] Hellman countered that barrel-aged whiskey "contain[ed] a large and dangerous percentage of fusel oil, a deadly poison, and a large percentage of other dangerous and deleterious impurities," that it was "unwholesome and impure," that Gaines failed to remove "dangerous and deleterious impurities" by a "process of rectification, blending, or vatting," and that, therefore, Gaines was "guilty of fraud upon the public."[20]

More was on the line than "just" a trademark. Despite the victories for producers of straight whiskey with the Bottled-in-Bond Act of 1897, the Pure Food and Drug Act of 1906, and the Taft Decision of 1909, rectifiers were *still* challenging straight whiskey producers. This made the lawsuits between Hellman and Gaines a true heavyweight battle, involving back-and-forth victories, numerous appeals, reversals, and efforts by Gaines to game the legal system.

The trademark aspect of the fight seemed clear: Hellman used the brand names Old Crow, Celebrated Old Crow, J. W. Crow, and P. Crow, which would cause obvious confusion with Old Crow produced by Gaines. If Hellman's use of the same and similar names was not enough, Hellman also used a logo depicting a crow perched on a whiskey barrel (fig. 9).[21] With its litigation success against "White Crow" (in *Leslie*) and "Crow" (in *Whyte Grocery*), Gaines must have thought that a trademark lawsuit against Hellman would result in a quick, decisive victory.

The first of many court decisions would have supported any such preconceived notions. In *W. A. Gaines & Co. v. Kahn* Gaines won the critical first battle.[22] Although the court recognized that Hellman had used versions of the Crow name since 1863 for its blended whiskey,[23] the court ruled that Hellman had done so fraudulently and to deceive its customers: "I am satisfied that this was done by them for the purpose of deceiving their customers as to the character of the whisky offered by them. They marked the barrels 'Crow,' and also used a picture of the bird on some of the packages. It was an attempt to palm off on the trade an inferior whisky, made under the name of 'Crow'; they well knowing at the time the superior quality of the whisky manufactured on Glenn's Creek, in Woodford county, Ky. It was unfair competition, in that they sought to make others believe that they were selling the genuine 'Old Crow' whisky, when, in fact, they were offering an inferior production of their own."[24]

The court also scoffed at Hellman's argument that it should be allowed to use the varieties of J. W. Crow and P. Crow because those names are not identical to Old Crow.[25] No person by those names or

FIG. 9. Celebrated Old Crow advertisement, I. & L. M. Hellman Co. *Kahn v. W. A. Gaines & Co.*, 1908.

initials had ever worked for Hellman, so the court would not allow Hellman to so easily skirt the trademarked name owned by Gaines.[26]

Hellman appealed, however, and the Circuit Court of Appeals for the Eighth Circuit sided with Hellman. In *Kahn v. W. A. Gaines & Co.* the court of appeals fixated on Hellman's use of the Crow name in 1863 and an initial 1882 trademark filing by Gaines that inexplicably identified its first use of the Crow name as 1870.[27] More specifically, the court of appeals was troubled by a second trademark registration filed by Gaines in June 1904—after the controversy had arisen between Gaines and Hellman but just before Gaines actually sued Hellman—in which Gaines backdated its use of the Crow name.[28] In that second trademark filing Gaines swore that its Crow trademark had actually been used continuously since 1835, not 1870, as previously asserted to the Trademark and Patent Office.

Focusing on this singular detail, the court of appeals ruled that "no unprejudiced mind can read the evidence in this case without the impression that the conception of a trade-mark in the words 'Crow,' or 'Old Crow,' did not enter the minds of Gaines, Berry & Co. prior to 1870."[29] Never mind that Gaines had actually used the Old Crow name before 1870, while it leased the Old Oscar Pepper Distillery; never mind that the 1882 trademark application related only to the name of the new distillery just built by Gaines (the Old Crow Distillery); and never mind that the 1904 trademark application, for the first time, referred to the predecessors to Gaines, from which Gaines had acquired rights to the Old Crow name.

In addition to the disappointingly myopic approach taken by the court of appeals, it also serves as an example of the evolution of trademark law and inconsistencies of the courts. The court of appeals was stuck in an old frame of mind that required proof of *actual confusion* to support this type of trademark claim, and therefore it was important to the court that Hellman had never represented that its whiskey was made on Glenn's Creek and never claimed to use "Kentucky corn, water, or air in the composition of their blended whisky."[30] Similarly, the court of appeals considered that no customer of Hellman had ever complained about being confused or about being deceived regarding whose whiskey was being sold.[31] Unfortunately for Gaines, the Eighth Circuit was behind the times. An earlier bourbon lawsuit out of the Sixth Circuit Court of Appeals, *Kentucky Distilleries & Warehouse Co. v. Wathen*,[32] had already held that actual confusion was not required in this type of trademark claim, but it was too late for Gaines.

When the Supreme Court of the United States refused to hear an appeal of the Missouri case, Gaines did the next best thing: it sued Hellman's Kentucky agent and distiller in Kentucky (outside of the unfriendly Eighth Circuit), the Rock Spring Distilling Company, again alleging trademark infringement. Hellman tried to impose itself as a party in the new Kentucky lawsuit, in order to argue that the issue had already been decided in Missouri, but the court rejected that effort.[33]

BEYOND BOURBON

"I WILL" versus "I Already Did"

Just like I. & L. M. Hellman Company defended against W. A. Gaines & Company by arguing that it was the first to use versions of the Crow name for whiskey, even though Gaines had registered the trademark first, this defense is alive and well today. Under Armour, a growing athletic apparel company making major inroads against market leaders Adidas and Nike, launched a global marketing campaign in 2013 with the slogan "I WILL," which it claimed to have used since 1998. Soon thereafter, Under Armour sued Nike for trademark infringement based upon Nike's campaign built around phrases beginning with "I will." Nike responded that this common phrase could not be protected as a trademark and, in any event, that *it* had used the phrase as early as 1995, before Under Armour's founding in 1996. Under Armour and Nike ultimately settled in 2014. *Under Armour, Inc. v. Nike, Inc.*, No. 1:13-cv-00571-ELH, 2014 WL 3810239 (D. Md. Feb. 10, 2014), Stipulated Dismissal of Complaint and Counterclaims.

Gaines also filed a new trademark application in July 1909 (after losing in the Eighth Circuit), this time limiting its use of the Old Crow name to "Straight Bourbon and Rye Whisky."[34] Substantively, though, the Kentucky court ultimately ruled that the trademark issue had been decided by the Eighth Circuit court of appeals and the slightly revised trademark application could not be used to override the Eighth Circuit's decision.[35] The court also found it "altogether incorrect" for Gaines to have asserted, in its 1909 trademark application, that it had used the Old Crow name since 1835 because the actual year of first use was 1867.[36] Similarly, the court ruled that it was "altogether incorrect" for Gaines to have asserted that no other similar trademark had been used by anyone else, when Gaines—at the very least because of the Missouri lawsuit—*knew* that Hellman had been using the Crow name since 1863.[37] Therefore, the court dismissed the new Kentucky lawsuit.

Still not deterred, Gaines appealed to the Sixth Circuit Court of Appeals, and this time Gaines won.[38] The Sixth Circuit held that the new trademark registration applied only to "straight" bourbon and rye whiskey, and therefore it was proper and enforceable by Gaines.[39] The court also ruled that there was no conflict with the 1908 ruling of the Eighth Circuit because that court did not award any affirmative trademark rights to Hellman, instead ruling simply that Hellman had a valid *defense* to the claims of infringement by Gaines.[40]

The Sixth Circuit was clearly troubled by the deceptive use by Hellman of the names J. W. Crow and P. Crow because, by 1863, the real Dr. Crow "Old Crow" had been produced since 1835 and was "considerably known on the market."[41] Either the initials meant nothing, posed the Sixth Circuit, or they were intended to deceive: "Witnesses for the defense frankly stated that in those years it was nothing unusual for jobbers or blenders of whisky to use well-known brands belonging to others, and that, if the initial of a proper name was changed, this was thought sufficient in morals to remove any objection to the appropriation. This may be the genesis of the otherwise unexplained use of 'P.' and 'J. W.'"[42]

The deception by Hellman, and the new limited use of the Old Crow name by Gaines to apply only to straight bourbon and rye whiskey, satisfied the Sixth Circuit that Rock Spring (and therefore Hellman) should be prevented from using the Crow name for any straight whiskies.[43] This was not the last chapter, however, because the Supreme Court of the United States decided to hear an appeal of this Sixth Circuit decision.

In *Rock Spring Distilling Co. v. W. A. Gaines & Co.* Gaines finally lost the Hellman lawsuit.[44] Without much explanation, the United States Supreme Court ruled that separate trademarks for "straight" whiskey and "blended" whiskey could not be maintained and that Hellman—not Gaines—owned the trademark rights to the Crow name.[45] In a twist of fate, however, this inauspicious end for Gaines would have spelled disaster but for Prohibition. The Supreme Court's decision was issued on March 18, 1918, exactly three months after the Eighteenth Amendment was proposed by the Senate.[46] Not even a year later, on January 16, 1919, the thirty-sixth state approved the Eighteenth Amendment, thus ratifying it, and the Volstead Act was then passed in October 1919.[47] Prohibition put Hellman out of business when Gaines could not, which allowed Old Crow to survive through Gaines, as aging stock and brand rights were acquired by the American Medicinal Spirits Company.

Since those pre-Prohibition days, Old Crow has been relatively silent in litigation until recently, when its current owner sought to make the brand edgy and relevant. This recent litigation also highlights another American tradition: self-regulation to avoid expanded governmental regulation. Today brands are constrained by agreement under the advertising rules of the national trade association the Distilled Spirits Council. In addition to advocacy on legislative, regulatory, and public affairs issues, DISCUS and its members have agreed to a Code of Responsible Practices for Beverage Alcohol Advertising and Marketing.

This DISCUS Code found its way into a trademark dispute between Wild Turkey (at the time using the corporate name of Rare Breed Distilling LLC) and Jim Beam (now Beam Suntory), in a case called *Rare Breed Distilling LLC v. Jim Beam Brands Co.*,[48] in order to stop Beam from using the slogan "Give 'em the Bird" for its Old Crow brand. Wild Turkey had used the registered mark "The Bird Is the Word" since the 1970s, and "the Bird" was commonly used to identify Wild Turkey bourbon.[49] Wild Turkey claimed that

Wild Turkey

Lawrenceburg, Kentucky

Rare Breed Kentucky Straight Bourbon Whiskey

Age: Unstated (blend of 6-, 8-, and 12-year-old bourbon)

Proof: 108.2 proof

Cost: $38.00–$48.00

Notes: Wild Turkey created Rare Breed as a relatively large batch, which has therefore provided more consistency for consumers over the years. While starting with caramel sweetness, Rare Breed shifts gears pretty quickly with a kick of spice and a hint of citrus. This 108.2 proof batch (WT-03RB), which ceased in 2014, is worth finding on the back of some out-of-the-way store shelf. Subsequent batches have steadily increased in proof but are not nearly as flavorful.

---

the public had adopted the Bird as a nickname for Wild Turkey bourbon, which gave Wild Turkey trademark rights, just like Volkswagen has rights to "the Bug" even though the official name of its iconic car is the Beetle.[50] Wild Turkey used a variety of slogans in the mid-2000s, such as "The only time to give a biker the Bird," "Give them the Bird," "Give 'em the Bird," and "Shoot the Bird."[51] Wild Turkey also submitted exhibits to show the prior use of "Give them the bird" and "Give 'em the Bird" (figs. 10 and 11).[52]

Of course, as the original iconic brand, Old Crow has a substantially longer history of association with a bird and bird imagery, so in March 2010 Beam applied to register the trademark "Give 'em the Bird."[53] Beam then rolled out a new, edgy branding campaign for Old Crow Reserve using this slogan (fig. 12).[54] The press release from Beam's marketing firm explained that Beam wanted to showcase the rich heritage of Old Crow along with "a touch of outlaw spirit" in the "rough and tumble market for bourbon whiskey."[55] In October 2010 Wild Turkey learned about the planned "outlaw spirit" campaign for Old Crow, so it sent a demand letter to Beam

FIG. 10. Wild Turkey "Give Them the Bird" advertisement (2006). *Rare Breed Distilling LLC v. Jim Beam Brands Co.*, 2011.

trying to protect its own marketing strategy, but Beam held firm on its Old Crow marketing plans.[56]

In the meantime Wild Turkey was in the midst of launching its own marketing campaign based on the "Give 'em the Bird" slogan, complete with Jimmy and Eddie Russell proudly extending their middle fingers for photo opportunities. As neither company backed off, in May 2011 Wild Turkey sued Beam in federal court in Louisville.[57] Beam countersued in June 2011, asking the court to immediately stop Wild Turkey from infringing on Beam's trademark

FIG. 11. Wild Turkey "Give 'Em the Bird" advertisement (2007). *Rare Breed Distilling LLC v. Jim Beam Brands Co.*, 2011.

because the "Give 'em the Bird" mark had just been granted registration by the U.S. Patent and Trademark Office on June 7, 2011.[58]

When the parties arrived at court for an injunction hearing in
July 2011, Beam relied on its trademark registration as the legal basis
to rule in its favor.[59] The parties presented arguments to the court
about their legal positions and precedent, but ultimately, because
the court wanted to hear evidence, not just legal arguments, the
parties scheduled another hearing for August 10, 2011.[60] Five days
before the hearing, Wild Turkey filed an extensive brief supporting
its position and also attached a survey that found that 24 percent of
the participants recognized the Bird as a Wild Turkey name, whereas
only 0.5 percent thought that it was associated with Old Crow.[61]

Before the hearing was conducted, however, the parties agreed to
dismiss all of their respective claims.[62] This agreement was probably
not so much about either side conceding but, instead, the result of
a ruling by DISCUS that the "Give 'em the Bird" campaign violated
the Code of Responsible Practices applicable to advertising because
its implicit vulgarity did not "reflect generally accepted contempo-

FIG. 12. Old Crow Reserve "Give 'Em the Bird" home page. *Rare Breed Distilling LLC v. Jim Beam Brands Co.*, 2011.

rary standards of good taste" and because advertising "should not contain any lewd or indecent images or language."[63] So, the "Give 'em the Bird" campaign was abandoned by both sides, and the trademark issue was never ruled upon.

This likely is not the final chapter for the once-famous Old Crow brand. Today the distilling equipment at the Old Crow Distillery (still owned by Beam Suntory) on Glenn's Creek sits idle, while the massive warehouses provide much-needed space for aging Beam Suntory's largest supply of bourbon in the world. And Old Crow continues to hold its spot at the bottom of Beam Suntory's lineup, while the company focuses on its core brands like Jim Beam (the world's best-selling bourbon), Booker's, and Knob Creek. If bourbon's history of resurgence provides any guidance, however, there is *always* a chance for rebirth. Especially in today's climate of sourced bourbon that lacks real history, Old Crow could reclaim its title as the most famous bourbon in the world.

FIVE

Bourbon Expands Trade Name Rights

Bourbon making has been a skill and tradition passed down within families, with brands often named after the actual historical people who first distilled or owned the brand. Eventually, as a family tree grows, not everyone in it can work for the family distillery, or family members otherwise decide to strike out on their own. One of the most prolific bourbon families has been the Beams, beginning with Jacob Beam in the late 1700s and continuing through Fred Noe today. But there are also Beams at other Kentucky distilleries. Joseph L. Beam was an original founder of Heaven Hill along with the Shapira family, which eventually bought him out, although he remained as the master distiller, followed by Harry Beam, Earl Beam, Parker Beam, and Craig Beam. Additionally, brothers Steve and Paul Beam started Limestone Branch Distillery, where they have the added distilling history on their mother's side of the once-famous Dant family and have now resurrected the Yellowstone brand.

But consumers will never see a label from Heaven Hill or Limestone Branch emphasizing the Beam name because bourbon litigation helped establish American law regarding whether and when a surname can be used in business or as a brand name. Similarly, bourbon lawsuits also helped expand trademark law to similar names about which customers were not necessarily confused. Finally, a case involving the world-famous Churchill Downs and a bourbon brand that wanted to capitalize on its good name helped extend trademark rights across lines of business.

A Kentucky bourbon lawsuit involving the once-famous Waterfill & Frazier brand is one of the earliest-known examples of American law prohibiting the use of one's own surname in business. As explained in *Frazier v. Dowling*, this case involved family drama plus the common theme of bourbon distillers trying to benefit from the established name of another brand.[1]

The Waterfill family had been in the distilling business since the early 1800s in Tyrone, Kentucky (in Anderson County, near Lawrenceburg).[2] William J. Waterfill and R. H. Frazier founded the Waterfill & Frazier Distillery in 1870 in Anderson County, Kentucky, with each owning one-half of the distillery.[3] In 1882 Waterfill sold his interest to Frazier, who continued the business.[4] But only three years later, in January 1885, R. H. Frazier wanted to sell, so William Waterfill partnered with John Dowling to purchase the distillery and the exclusive right to the brand name Waterfill & Frazier.[5] In addition, Dowling paid William Waterfill three hundred dollars to use the Waterfill name.[6]

R. H. Frazier died soon afterward, and his son, Grant G. Frazier, perhaps being disappointed in not having inherited the distillery, decided to start his own distillery with James M. Waterfill, a cousin of William Waterfill.[7] This next generation of the Waterfills and Fraziers built their new distillery only a few miles away from the original in Anderson County in 1890 and were able to begin distilling that fall, barreling their own Waterfill & Frazier bourbon.[8]

William Waterfill, of course, was still an owner of the original Waterfill & Frazier Distillery.[9] He made clear to brokers that only he and Dowling could use the Waterfill & Frazier brand, and he expressed his confidence that "any court of jurisdiction will protect us in the right of property in that brand," in a letter intended to prevent the upstarts from finding a sales outlet for their competing whiskey (fig. 13).[10]

This brushback pitch convinced the young entrepreneurs to brand their barrels "J. M. Waterfill & Company, Distillers" and to change their advertisements to clarify that their distillery was owned by "G. G. Frazier" and "J. M. Waterfill."[11] But only a few months later, on September 1, 1890, Dowling bought out William Waterfill for

All in the Family

Bourbon might have been the earliest industry to have family members competing with each other and all wanting to use the family surname, and bourbon law helped set the guidelines for later cases. Ernest & Julio Gallo Winery is a famous California winery with wine family drama every bit as sensational as bourbon family drama. Brothers Ernest and Julio started their winery from practically nothing while they were guardians over their younger brother, Joseph. Amid claims by Joseph that his older brothers had cheated him out of his share of the inheritance and misused his stock while he was a minor, Joseph left the family business and became a successful rancher and dairy farmer, ultimately selling cheeses under the Gallo name. Ernest and Julio sued their younger brother for trademark infringement and dilution. Joseph lost and was prohibited from using the Gallo name for the retail sale of cheese, although he could still use it for wholesale packages and as a trade name for his farm. *E. & J. Gallo Winery v. Gallo Cattle Co.*, 1989 WL 159628 (E.D. Cal. 1989) *aff'd* 955 F.2d 1327 (9th Cir. 1992), opinion amended and superseded, 967 F.2d 1280 (9th Cir. 1992).

---

seventeen thousand dollars, which included the exclusive right to use the Waterfill & Frazier brand name.[12] William Waterfill then partnered with the younger Waterfill and Frazier.[13] So, the original Waterfill & Frazier Distillery was now owned solely by Dowling, with no person named Waterfill or Frazier associated with the distillery.[14]

In the meantime the younger Waterfill and Frazier had been unable to sell their whiskey.[15] But now with the help of William Waterfill, they finally found a broker in Chicago who agreed to buy all of their whiskey—so long as they would label it as "Waterfill & Frazier."[16] Accordingly, they began advertising their own whiskey as "Waterfill & Frazier" (fig. 14).[17]

When Dowling learned that the upstarts were using the Waterfill & Frazier brand name, he started his own advertising campaign,

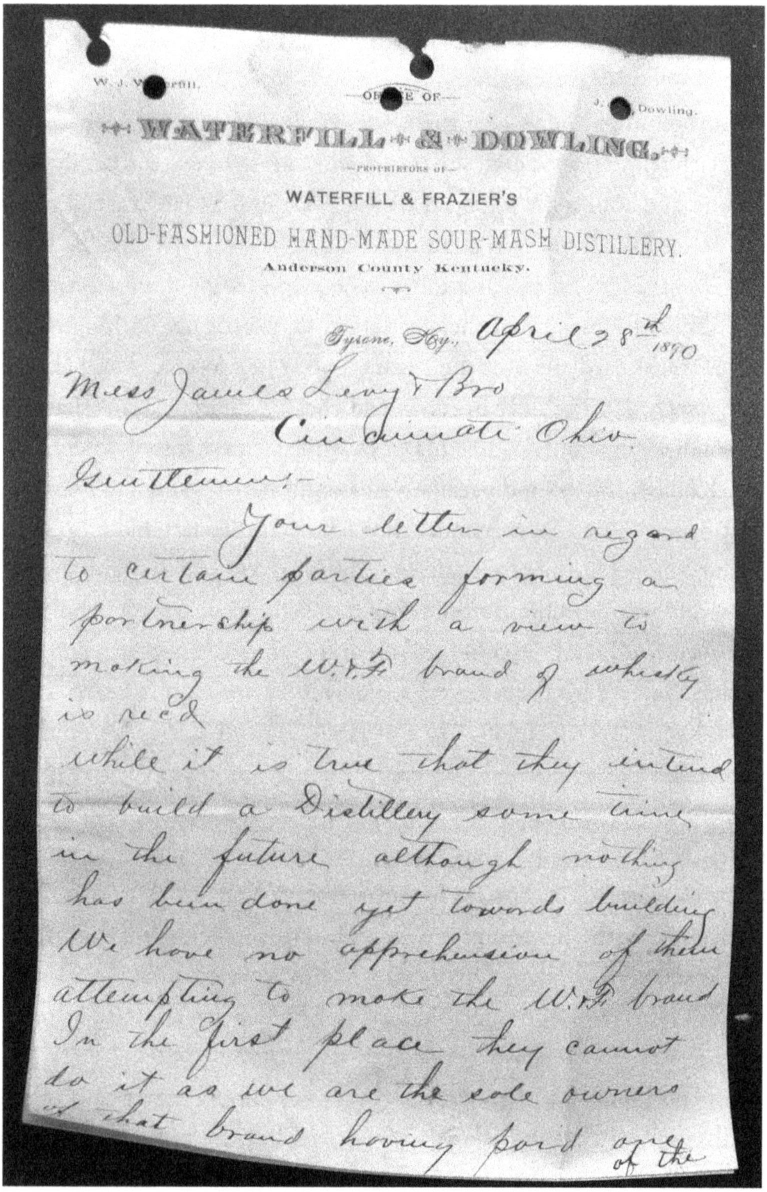

W. J. W erfill. — OF E OF — J. Dowling.

WATERFILL & DOWLING,

—PROPRIETORS OF—

WATERFILL & FRAZIER'S

OLD-FASHIONED HAND-MADE SOUR-MASH DISTILLERY.

Anderson County Kentucky.

Tyrone, Ky., April 28th 1890

Mess James Levy & Bro
Cincinnati Ohio

Gentlemen:-

Your letter in regard to certain parties forming a partnership with a view to making the W.&F. brand of whisky is rec'd

While it is true that they intend to build a Distillery some time in the future although nothing has been done yet towards building We have no apprehension of their attempting to make the W.&F. brand In the first place they cannot do it as we are the sole owners of that brand having paid one of the

FIG. 13. Letter from William J. Waterfill to Cincinnati whiskey brokers, April 28, 1890. *Frazier v. Dowling*, 1897; *John Dowling v. G. G. Frazier*, 1892. Kentucky State Archives.

FIG. 14. *Wine and Spirit Bulletin* Waterfill & Frazier advertisement for G. G. Frazier and J. M. Waterfill. *Frazier v. Dowling*, 1897; *John Dowling v. G. G. Frazier*. Kentucky State Archives.

complete with a prevalent warning (fig. 15).[18] Dowling also sued and obtained an injunction, but the Fraziers and Waterfills appealed.[19] The Court of Appeals of Kentucky agreed with the trial court and ruled against the young Fraziers and Waterfills, prohibiting them from using their own last names for their whiskey brand because, it said, they were trying to deceive the public.[20] Dowling and the Waterfill & Frazier brand continued to prosper, while the upstarts faded into obscurity.

This 1897 case is one of the first rulings that prohibited the use of one's own surname, but it was by no means the last. It laid the groundwork for an exception to the rule that people have the right to use their own name in their own business: they cannot use their own name if it would create market confusion. This exception arose again in bourbon legal history in a 1940 decision involving a rush to open distilleries after Repeal of National Prohibition. One of the many casualties of Prohibition was a massive distillery complex nestled in a scenic bend on the meandering Elkhorn Creek near Frankfort, Kentucky. Now owned by Beam Suntory, it is only used for aging and bottling, but it has a rich history dating back to 1901, when R. A. Baker established the Frankfort Distillery, extending through to 1940–87, when it was home to the famous Old Grand-

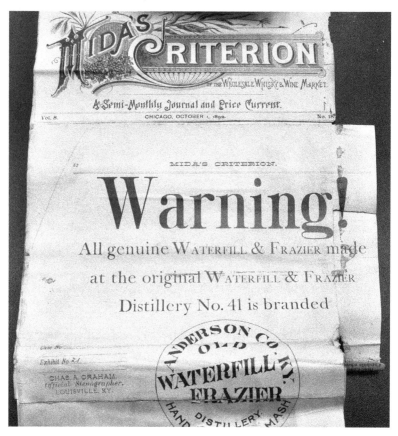

FIG. 15. *Mida's Criterion* Waterfill & Frazier advertisement for John Dowling. *Frazier v. Dowling*, 1897; *John Dowling v. G. G. Frazier*. Kentucky State Archives.

Dad brand. The case of *National Distillers Products Corp. v. K. Taylor Distilling Co.* tells the story of the post-Prohibition revival of the Frankfort Distillery.[21]

The court began its story with a summary of how Col. E. H. Taylor Jr. and his sons, Swigert and Kenner, organized "E. H. Taylor, Jr. & Sons" in 1877 in Millville, Kentucky, and how the Old Taylor brand rose to great prominence.[22] Old Taylor became a popular brand in part because of extensive advertising *outside* of Kentucky.[23] In a remarkable feat for the time, it was estimated that up through 1923, the Old Taylor Distillery had produced and sold fifty million bottles of Old Taylor.[24] The Old Taylor brand became so well-known that the word *Taylor* developed its own secondary meaning as the whiskey produced in Millville by E. H. Taylor, Jr. & Sons.[25] The court also explained that when Colonel Taylor died, in 1923, his sons basically wasted no time in selling out to what eventually became part of National Distillers Products Corporation.[26]

As the demise of National Prohibition became more likely, speculators positioned themselves to enter the market.[27] One of those entrepreneurs was a Lexington, Kentucky, attorney, S. S. Yantis, who, along with his New York City investment banker relatives, thought the timing was right to invest in a distillery.[28] Before Repeal they bought "a former distillery site located near Forks of Elkhorn in Franklin County, Ky. . . . with the view of promoting an enterprise for the manufacture of whiskey in the event of the repeal of National Prohibition, which seemed impending."[29] Four months before Repeal, they formed the Franklin County Distilling Company and began preparations to reopen the distillery.[30]

The court noted that the Yantis family was "entirely without previous experience in the distillery business," so they courted two other prominent former distillers, who rejected them, before approaching Kenner Taylor.[31] In September 1933 Kenner Taylor agreed to become president and CEO of the new company for a five-year term, and he agreed that his name could be used for branding and advertising purposes.[32]

With the instant prestige afforded by Taylor's participation, in October 1933 the two-month-old company changed its name to the K. Taylor Distilling Company.[33] Repeal came on December 5, 1933, and later that month Taylor left for Florida for his usual winter vacation. Taylor returned to Kentucky on April 1, 1934, but he was ill, and on June 1 he died.[34] While the company never actually distilled any whiskey during Taylor's brief stint as president, he assisted in launching the Kenner Taylor brand using sourced bourbon.[35]

After Taylor's death, the company ramped up use of the Taylor name—but not just that of Kenner Taylor.[36] Instead, the court noted that the company advertised by using pictures of E. H. Taylor Jr.,

Swigert Taylor, and Kenner Taylor and employed the phrase *Taylor-Made Whiskies*.[37] The court held that this use infringed on the Old Taylor brand because it misled the public into believing that the K. Taylor brand was related to Old Taylor.[38] Therefore, the court prohibited use of the brand name K. Taylor or Kenner Taylor "unless accompanied by a statement plainly and specifically showing that the defendant is neither the successor to nor connected with the maker of 'Old Taylor whiskey' and that its product is 'not the product of E. H. Taylor, Jr. & Sons, or its successors.'"[39]

The ruling was issued on February 14, 1940, and the K. Taylor Distilling Company fought on by challenging National Distillers in the marketplace. A mere month after the ruling, in March 1940, the company contracted with a Cincinnati distributor that successfully developed a demand for "K. Taylor, Bottled-in-Bond" and somewhat less demand for a second K. Taylor brand called the "Belle of Franklin."[40]

Having won its lawsuit but seemingly having failed to destroy the K. Taylor Distilling Company, on August 5, 1940, National Distillers bought the upstart distillery along with the K. Taylor brand, which it immediately discontinued.[41] National Distillers then rechristened the distillery as the "Old Grand-Dad Distillery," making one of the most popular brands of the time and following in the American way of buying out a troublesome competitor.

To the contrary, another example of bourbon law expanding protection of trademarks and trade names shows how trademark law can lead to innovation and the creation of a new iconic brand. *Country Distillers Products, Inc. v. Samuels, Inc.* tells the background story of what became the current-day Maker's Mark.[42] The court began by noting that the Samuels family had been making whiskey for over one hundred years at the time of this lawsuit but had not incorporated its distillery until 1933, when it formed the T. W. Samuels Distillery (named after Taylor William Samuels, the original Samuels commercial distiller) with other corporate investors.[43] The name was changed to Country Distillers Products, Inc., in January 1942, and the distillery continued to produce the T. W. Samuels and Old

Jim Beam

Clermont, Kentucky

Old Grand-Dad Bottled in Bond Kentucky Straight Bourbon Whiskey

Age: Unstated (but at least 4 years)

Proof: 100 proof

Cost: $17.00

Notes: Beam uses a high-rye mash bill for the Old Grand-Dad (offered at different proof levels) and Basil Hayden's (offered only at 80 proof) brands, and it is evident, creating a swell of rye spice to complement flavors of sweet corn, butterscotch, and cinnamon, along with telltale Beam orange citrus. Old Grand-Dad is a well-balanced, robust bourbon that deserves attention.

Jordan brands.[44] Beginning on October 6, 1942, however, all whiskey production was halted in United States in order to support the war effort.[45]

About eighteen months after the official name change, on July 30, 1943, Taylor William "Bill Sr." Samuels IV, the great-grandson of T. W. Samuels, resigned and sold all of his shares in the company.[46] Bill Sr. was far too young to retire; he planned on making better bourbon, so a mere six weeks later—on September 14, 1943— he incorporated Old Samuels Distillery, Inc., and T. W. Samuels, Inc., resulting in an inevitable lawsuit filed by Country Distillers.[47] Duty called, though, and Bill Sr. joined the army in 1944.[48] Bill Sr. served during World War II until being honorably discharged on December 27, 1945.[49] Between the war, his service, and the lawsuit, Bill Sr. had not taken any steps to build a distillery, nor had he applied for any permits or licenses,[50] leaving Country Distillers with seemingly little to complain about. And as for the usage of his own name, when confronted by Country Distillers, Bill Sr. testified that he only wanted to use his name as a corporate name and not for a brand name, but Country Distillers wanted to completely prohibit Bill Sr.'s use of his own name.[51]

The trial court ruled that while Bill Sr. could use the name T. W. Samuels, Inc., as a company name, the Samuels name could not be emphasized on labels, nor could he use Samuels or Old Samuels as brand names, and he also had to include the phrase "not connected with Country Distillers, Inc." on each label.[52] In a 1948 decision the Court of Appeals of Kentucky mostly agreed with the trial court. While the court recognized that so long as people do not create confusion in the market, they always have the "undeniable right" to use their own name in their own business, in this case the name T. W. Samuels *did* create confusion.[53] So, the court affirmed the restriction on the font size of using the corporate names on labels and against using T. W. Samuels as a brand name and the disclaimer that it was "not connected with Country Distillers."[54] Probably because Bill Sr. had been willing to provide this disclaimer all along, the court of appeals ordered Country Distillers to pay his costs.

But American law also prides itself on equitable exceptions to exceptions, as bourbon law also made clear in *John P. Dant Distillery Co. v. Schenley Distillers, Inc.*[55] Once a prominent bourbon family, the Dant brand had become splintered by the mid-twentieth century. The Dant family traces its distilling roots to 1836 with Joseph Washington Dant, the namesake of the famed J. W. Dant brand.[56] Joseph Dant had seven sons, two of whom—John P. Dant Sr. and George Washington Dant—were instrumental in continuing the family business.[57] John Sr. operated the John P. Dant Distillery Company, Inc., at the Meadowlawn Distillery near Louisville, while George operated the J. W. Dant Distillery (changed in 1897 to the Dant Distillery Co., Inc.) in Dant, Kentucky.[58] John Sr. was succeeded by his son John P. Dant Jr., while the much larger Dant Distillery Company was sold to United Distillers of America, Inc., after George died, which then was acquired by Schenley Distillers, Inc., in 1953.[59] When each Dant distillery was owned by Dant family members, they cooperated, and both used the Dant name in their brands.[60] It was not until Schenley arrived that it threatened John P. Dant Jr. and sought exclusive use of the Dant name.

Luxco and Limestone Branch

St. Louis, Missouri (Luxco)

Bardstown, Kentucky (Lux Row Distillers)

Lebanon, Kentucky (Limestone Branch)

Yellowstone 2015 Limited Edition Kentucky Straight Bourbon Whiskey

Age: Blend of 12-year, 7-year, and 7-year bourbon

Proof: 105 proof

Cost: $105.00

Notes: Limestone Branch is led by descendants of both the Beam and Dant families, Steve and Paul Beam, and their partnership with Luxco has given them access to a wide supply of sourced bourbon. Like some limited editions offered by Luxco, the Yellowstone Limited Edition bourbons have blended bourbon of different ages and different mash bills (using wheat and rye as secondary grains). The aromas and flavors are rich, with buttery caramel and vanilla as well as fresh clover, creamed corn, cinnamon, oak, leather, and slight mint.

After acknowledging the general rule that "every man has the undeniable right to the use of his patronymic name in his business and he cannot be absolutely restrained from using it, even though another person bearing the same name, previously established in a business of the same character, has adopted it," and the exception to the rule that restricts the use of a surname whenever it would cause confusion, the court formulated an equitable exception to the exception.[61] Because both sides of the Dant family had used the Dant name as part of their business and brand names and neither tried to restrict the other for over forty years, Schenley could not swoop in to claim an exclusive right to the Dant name.[62]

A second topic of trademark expansion impelled by a bourbon lawsuit involved the Wathen family and brand and clarified that *actual consumer confusion* is not required in some circumstances. While there is no Wathen distillery today (the Wathen brand name remains as a sourced bourbon), members of the Wathen family were whiskey pioneers in Kentucky, and they have litigation history spanning the period from the late 1800s through the post-Prohibition era, documenting their legacy, which involves their survival during Prohibition as part of the American Medicinal Spirits Company (AMS).

Henry Hudson Wathen (1756–1851) settled seven miles south of Lebanon, Kentucky, in 1788. Two years later, in 1790, he started a "very small and crude distillery" according to a family history published in a 1905 edition of the *Wine and Spirit Bulletin*.[63] In 1852 Henry's youngest son, Richard Bernard Wathen (1815–80), started his own distillery just about one mile from Henry's distillery.[64] Richard had five sons who eventually worked in the distilling business, the most prolific of whom was John Bernard "J.B." Wathen (1844–1919).[65] The other brothers were Richard Nicholas "Nick", Martin Athanasius "Nace," William H., and John A.[66] In turn J.B.'s most prolific distilling son was Richard Eugene "Dick" Wathen, although most of his brothers and other sons were also involved in the family business.[67]

J.B. moved to Louisville and built the J. B. Wathen & Brother Distillery in 1880 with his brother William. Their brother Nace joined them in 1881, and by 1885 the brothers rolled the partnership into a corporation called "J. B. Wathen & Bros. Company."[68] The Wathen brothers experienced incredible success and reinvested in the company by installing one of the first continuous column stills in Kentucky and installing steam heat in the warehouses.[69] John A. Wathen joined his brothers in 1887 to manage the company.[70]

J.B. sold J. B. Wathen & Bros. Company to the infamous Kentucky Distilleries & Warehouse Company (the Kentucky Whiskey Trust) in the spring of 1899.[71] John A. Wathen stayed with the Kentucky Whiskey Trust as an employee.[72] In the meantime the family's other distilleries stayed in the family.[73] J. B. Wathen found himself in an immediate dispute with the Kentucky Whiskey Trust: he sold his distillery on April 13, 1899, but negotiated to continue operations until June 1, 1899.[74] The Kentucky Whiskey Trust agreed to

Wathen's

Owensboro, Kentucky

Wathen's Kentucky Straight Bourbon Whiskey

Age: Unstated

Proof: 94 proof

Cost: $40.00

Notes: While the source distillery has likely changed over the past years for Wathen's, this bourbon has tended to be more on the earthy, nutty side of the spectrum. Other "darker" flavors include raisin, plums, and clove, but it is not all dark; there is also a bit of vanilla, caramel, and citrus zest, although perhaps not enough to call it well balanced. Wathen's helps prove that not all bourbon is sweet.

---

continue to store "a large amount of whiskey"—some owned by J. B. Wathen, and some owned by others who held warehouse receipts from J.B.—including a guaranteed maximum loss due to evaporation or shrinkage. The Kentucky Whiskey Trust was negligent in its care of the barrels, resulting in astounding leakage and loss.[75] The Kentucky Whiskey Trust refused to pay for these losses, necessitating a lawsuit in April 1890 to enforce the contract payments.[76]

Perhaps J. B. Wathen took this personally because shortly thereafter—in a move that must have led to awkward dinner table discussions—J.B. orchestrated the formation of a new distilling company to compete against the Kentucky Whiskey Trust.[77] He named the new company "R. E. Wathen & Company" after his eldest son and used brand names that infringed on the brand names that J.B. had just sold to the Kentucky Whiskey Trust.[78] R. E. Wathen & Company employed former J. B. Wathen & Bros. Company employees, used the office space from which J.B. had run his company, and used J.B.'s equipment.[79]

The primary brands of J. B. Wathen & Bros. Company, which of course were sold to the Kentucky Whiskey Trust, were Ky. Criterion and Honeymoon and the distillery was sometimes known as the "West End Distillery."[80] The new R. E. Wathen & Company called its distillery the "East End Distillery" and promoted its brands as Ky. Credential and Honeycomb.[81] As might be expected, the Kentucky Whiskey Trust sued and asked for an injunction.[82]

Victoria's Secret versus Victor's Secret

In 1998 Victor Moseley opened a store in Elizabethtown, Kentucky, selling "adult" videos, risqué novelties, and lingerie under the name Victor's Secret. The well-known Victoria's Secret store took issue and sued under a number of trademark theories to prevent Moseley from using his own first name in conjunction with *Secret*. The federal district court granted an injunction to Victoria's Secret based upon the Federal Trademark Dilution Act of 1995, and after a decade of appeals—including a reversal by the United States Supreme Court—the injunction was ultimately sustained after Congress passed the Trademark Dilution Revision Act of 2006. The primary claim at issue was not necessarily that there was a likelihood of confusion between the semantically similar names but, instead, that Victor's Secret tarnished the Victoria's Secret trademark because of its association with risqué products.

Similar to the lack of consumer confusion needed in *Kentucky Distilleries & Warehouse Co. v. Wathen*, 110 F. 641, 645 (C.C. W.D. Ky. 1901), and the mere tendency to create confusion by using a famous surname in *National Distillers Products Corp. v. K. Taylor Distilling Co.*, 31 F. Supp. 611, 615 (E.D. Ky. 1940), Victoria's Secret only had to prove a likelihood of brand tarnishment instead of actual harm. *V Secret Catalogue, Inc. v. Moseley*, No. 3:98CV-395-S, 2000 WL 370525 (W.D. Ky. Feb. 9, 2000); *V Secret Catalogue, Inc. v. Moseley*, 259 F.3d 464 (6th Cir. 2001); *Moseley v. V Secret Catalogue, Inc.*, 537 U.S. 418 (2003); *V Secret Catalogue, Inc. v. Moseley*, 558 F. Supp. 2d 734 (W.D. Ky. 2008); *V Secret Catalogue, Inc. v. Moseley*, 605 F.3d 382 (6th Cir. 2010).

The court's July 16, 1901, ruling held that the two new brands unfairly infringed on the brands just acquired by the Kentucky Whiskey Trust, *even though consumers had not necessarily been deceived.*[83] The court noted that federal law had required, since 1892, that the name of the distiller be stamped or burned upon the head of every barrel of distilled spirits (hence the origin of the term *brand name*).[84] The court also noted that distillers sold their whiskey in barrel lots to wholesalers, and then it was sold by "drummers" to retailers, which then sold the whiskey to the public in bottles that did not necessarily include the brand name of the distiller.[85] The Kentucky Whiskey Trust apparently acknowledged that the wholesalers had not been misled by the similar names used by the new Wathen company, but in possibly the first extension of brand name rights, the court still enjoined the Wathens from using *Ky. Credential* and *Honeycomb* simply to protect the names acquired by the Kentucky Whiskey Trust.[86]

The Wathens were true Kentucky bourbon pioneers, and like so many of the colorful characters of bourbon legend, they had a maverick instinct and did not shy away from conflict. While the Kentucky Whiskey Trust won the fight in court, the Wathens outlived the trust, succeeded wildly with Old Grand-Dad and other brands, thrived during Prohibition, and are still memorialized in brands today.

The maverick instinct that led to the Wathens' success was probably part of why an upstart distiller decided to appropriate the Churchill Downs name for his bourbon—a move that would seem doomed from the start based upon today's standards. While this appropriation could have been legal in the early 1930s, *Churchill Downs Distilling Co. v. Churchill Downs, Inc.* established the right of owners to protect their trade names against use by anyone else, even in a different industry.[87]

It all started in 1933, when B. J. Frentz decided to get into the whiskey business by opening Churchill Downs Distilling Company in Nelson County, Kentucky, about thirty miles from Louisville.[88] (This distillery, in Boston, Kentucky, is now owned by Beam Suntory.) None of Frentz's business partners were named Churchill or Downs, and he had no connection whatsoever to the real Churchill Downs, but he used that name prominently on his bottles, along with identifying Louisville as his place of business.[89] His label included an image of the grandstand located at Churchill Downs, along with horses and jockeys racing on a track.[90]

The real Churchill Downs had never agreed to the use of its name in this manner.[91] Frentz even admitted in his testimony that he used the name Churchill Downs precisely because it was well-known and he hoped it would increase sales.[92] He admitted that there was no connection with the real Churchill Downs and that he was trying to profit from the reputation of Churchill Downs, which, since opening and featuring the first Kentucky Derby in 1875, had gained worldwide renown.[93]

Instead, Frentz argued that the law only protected the name Churchill Downs from use by horse track *competitors* and that a company's goodwill in its name only extended to its own actual line of business.[94] Since Frentz did not operate a horse racing track, he argued that he was free to use the name without permission or consequence.[95] But the court decided to adopt an emerging trend in the law that expanded the scope of protection for unfair competition, so that it was not confined to actual market competition.[96] Now the law would protect against use of a trade name by anyone else who tried to pass off his goods or services as being connected to or endorsed by that business.[97]

While American law has no doubt had its share of inequitable results, bourbon lawsuits have helped set the standard for the rule of law and, when necessary, equitable exceptions. Bourbon's many family dynasties make it the perfect test kitchen for finding the appropriate balance between naming rights and fair competition in the marketplace, and its mavericks helped test the parameters of trademark protection.

SIX

Bourbon Marketers Write the Book
on Puffery and Exaggeration

implex commendation non obligat is a maxim meaning, roughly, "simple commendations do not create obligations," and in the mid-1800s English courts ruled that such advertising "puff" could not lead to liability.[1] While the origin of the law of "puffery" was not rooted in bourbon lawsuits, it fits right into a proud tradition of bourbon marketing.

Essentially, puffing, or puffery, is an exaggerated or boastful advertising statement that requires no substantiation. It is a type of advertising that is more "blustering and boasting which no reasonable buyer would believe was true" and therefore is not actionable.[2] Puffing can be seen as sanctioned lying, as long as the lie is relatively non-specific and so exaggerated that no reasonable consumer would be wrongly influenced. Courts will also consider whether the advertising statement can be measured objectively. If it can be measured (like "voted the best bourbon in America") and if it is false, then the statement may cross the line into false advertising.

Generally speaking, courts hold that vague or subjective statements—ones that cannot be measured or proved false—are mere puffing instead of false advertising. Bourbon marketing history is filled to the brim with puffery, and occasionally courts have addressed whether or not puffery has crossed the line into false labeling. One of those cases involved the rush of brands seeking a foothold in the "super premium" market and the brand currently known simply as "1792 Small Batch," produced by Barton Distillery. The original brand name was Ridgewood Reserve, and Brown-Forman alleged that it infringed on its Woodford Reserve brand name, logo, trademarked label design, and flask-shaped bottle. The case took a turn into cross-allegations of misrepresentations to consumers, with Barton's alleged misrepresentation being that it lied to create a "legend" out of thin air.

In *Brown-Forman Corp. v. Barton Inc.* the evidence showed that the marketers for Barton decided that the best way for Barton to launch a new premium brand would be by "tying the product to geographic locations, historical figures or to bourbon history."[3] Since the word *Ridgewood* had no true meaning, the marketers "named" the existing still at the Barton Distillery the "Legendary Ridgewood Still."[4] Overnight the still became "legendary" and had a name, but it was a farce used to legitimize the Ridgewood Reserve name.[5] As part of its defense, Barton argued that calling the still legendary was mere puffery and that it could not be subject to any misrepresentation claims because of it.[6] The consumer misrepresentation claims were ultimately dropped by both parties, and Barton was forced to change the Ridgewood Reserve name on trademark infringement grounds.[7]

Another example of puffing is use of a word found on many bourbon labels: *handmade*. In the modern era there have always been steps in the bourbon-making process that have been done by machine. Indeed, as early as 1905, writers were lamenting that "'old fashioned hand-made sour mash whisky' will soon be a thing of the past" because of modern machinery: "The world over, Kentucky is famous for beautiful women, for fine horses, and for good whisky. And when Kentucky whisky is mentioned, it means Bourbon whisky. In the year 1902 to 1903, America produced a little over 26,000,000 gallons of Bourbon whisky, and of these 24,759,890 gallons were made in Kentucky. Pennsylvania and Maryland, Rye; but Kentucky, Bourbon. . . . The 'old fashioned hand-made sour mash whisky' will soon be a thing of the past. Modern machinery has largely supplanted the old-time mashing by hand, and large mashing tubs and fermenters the small one-bushel tubs."[8]

Now more than ever—and especially in distilleries that are more industrial than bucolic—bourbon may be fairly characterized as

Barton 1792

Bardstown, Kentucky

1792 Small Batch Kentucky Straight Bourbon Whiskey

Age: Unstated

Proof: 93.7 proof

Cost: $30.00–$40.00

Notes: This bourbon began as Ridgewood Reserve, was renamed Ridgemont Reserve after litigation with Brown-Forman, and has now been renamed again to simply 1792 Small Batch, invoking the year that Kentucky became the fifteenth state in the union. 1792 Small Batch has a prickly, firm spice to it, with dry oak, licorice, and cinnamon and with just slight caramel, maple sweetness, and light fruit flavors for balance. This is a popular bourbon, especially its "full proof" variety.

---

being "manufactured" in a highly mechanized and computerized process. Because of this mechanization, plaintiffs in California and Florida filed class action complaints against Maker's Mark in 2014 alleging that its use of the term *handmade* was false and misleading.

Maker's Mark was successful in having both cases dismissed, first the Florida case in May 2015. The court in *Salters v. Beam Suntory, Inc.* noted that there are different possible meanings for the word *handmade*: "The term 'handmade' goes back many years.[9] The original meaning was 'distinguished from the work of nature.'"[10] "In that sense all bourbon is handmade; bourbon, unlike coffee or orange juice, cannot be grown in the wild."[11] However, the court recognized that this particular usage of the word *handmade* is no longer common. Instead, the current definition of *handmade* is "made by hand."[12] That circular definition cannot literally describe how bourbon is made, since machines are involved in most steps along the way. As the court noted: "One can knit a sweater by hand, but one cannot make bourbon by hand. . . . No reasonable consumer could believe otherwise."[13]

Because no reasonable consumer could believe otherwise, the Florida plaintiffs tried to offer other possible meanings of *handmade* to create some sort of misrepresentation by Maker's Mark. For example, the plaintiffs argued that *handmade* means being "made from scratch or in small units," that it "implies close attention by a human being, not a high-volume, untended process," or that it suggests being "made with only some kinds of machines, not others . . . [such as] machines that are too big or too modern."[14] The court scoffed at these attempts too. If not taken literally—which it cannot be—then saying something is "handmade" is a general, undefined statement that is not actionable because it is puffery.[15]

A few months later a federal court in California issued a similar ruling.[16] The plaintiffs in *Nowrouzi v. Maker's Mark Distillery, Inc.* alleged that they bought Maker's Mark because the label contained the statement that it was handmade, allegedly leading them to believe that Maker's Mark "'was of superior quality' than other bourbon thus justifying spending more for defendant's product than other lesser quality products."[17] They alleged that they were misled because Maker's Mark's process "involves 'little to no human supervision, assistance or involvement' . . . [which is] 'mechanized and/or automated,'" contrary to the meaning of *handmade*, which "is defined in the Meridian [*sic*] Webster dictionary as 'created by hand process rather than a machine.'"[18]

Maker's Mark's first argument was that California law protected it from liability because the Alcohol and Tobacco Tax and Trade Bureau had approved its label.[19] In other words, Maker's Mark argued that, because it had complied with the federal regulations in the labeling process, because TTB is the federal agency charged with promulgating regulations regarding labeling of distilled spirits and other alcoholic beverages pursuant to the Federal Alcohol Administration Act (FAAA), and because TTB reviews and preapproves distilled spirits labels to ensure compliance with applicable laws (including whether the label is false or misleading), Maker's Mark should not be subject to liability for a consumer's claim related to labeling.[20]

Maker's Mark compared the label approval process to prescription drug labeling by the Food and Drug Administration (FDA) and food labeling by the U.S. Department of Agriculture (USDA), for which consumer claims based on labels are dismissed routinely in cases in which the federal regulatory agencies had approved the labels.[21] The court disagreed, however, because the TTB's approval of labels is an informal agency decision, unlike the stringent investigatory process used by the USDA and the FDA.[22] At the very least there was no proof that TTB had specifically investigated the "handmade" claim on the label, so the court had insufficient evidence to support a dismissal.[23]

While TTB approval may not necessarily give a producer license to put whatever it wants on a label, courts will still analyze whether label statements really cause a likelihood of deception among members of the public. "Likely to be deceived" means "more than a mere possibility of misunderstanding—'likelihood' is measured in terms of whether a significant portion of the general consumer public could be misled."[24] Maker's Mark argued that using *handmade* could not be misleading because it is not a "specific and measurable claim."[25] Rather than a factual representation, it is a general, subjective term that cannot be measured; in other words, using the word *handmade* is puffery.[26]

Handmade cannot mean that "Maker's Mark employees break up the grain with their hands, stir the mixture by hand, distill and ferment the alcohol without the use of any machine, make . . . glass bottles by hand, fill each bottle by hand, and handwrite the labels on the bottles."[27] The federal court in California agreed with the earlier decision by the federal court in Florida on the issue of puffery: "This Court finds that 'handmade' cannot reasonably be interpreted as meaning literally by hand nor that a reasonable consumer would understand the term to mean no equipment or automated process was used to manufacture the whisky."[28] *Handmade* is puffery, and puffery is allowed.

While these cases might encourage bourbon producers to engage in more puffery, other bourbon lawsuits show the downside to puffery, exaggeration, and tall tales. W. A. Gaines & Company learned

FIG. 16. Hermitage label script. *W. A. Gaines & Co. v. Turner-Looker Co.*, 1913.

this lesson the hard way, at just about the same time that it was learning hard lessons about its Old Crow brand. Gaines had another prominent brand in the late 1800s and early 1900s called "Hermitage." When faced with an imposter brand in California, Gaines sued, alleging that the competitor sold "a cheap imitation and inferior grade of whisky, in barrels which are labeled with false and misleading labels, having printed thereon the title 'Hermitage Whisky.'"[29] The court dismissed Gaines's complaint, however, because Gaines was not specific enough in its allegations.

Now, over one hundred years later, only speculation can provide reasons why Gaines failed to be more specific, but a second historical Hermitage case might provide the answer. In *W. A. Gaines & Co. v. Turner-Looker Co.* Gaines alleged with specificity both its own label usage and trademark of *Hermitage* and Turner-Looker's use of a name obviously similar to Gaines's trademarked name. Turner-Looker used the name Golden Heritage, which, standing alone, might not have seemed problematic. The problem arose from the similar font and style used by Turner-Looker. When comparing Gaines's trademarked name to Turner-Looker's similar name, all odds must have seemed to favor Gaines (figs. 16 and 17).[30]

Indeed, the court recognized that "the similarity in appearance is obvious."[31] Moreover, the court concluded that Turner-Looker's trade name "is calculated to deceive the public, and to enable the palming off of [its] goods as those of [Gaines]."[32] Even though the two brands had readily apparent differences—such as Hermitage being labeled "Kentucky Straight Bourbon Whisky," whereas Golden

FIG. 17. Golden Heritage label script. *W. A. Gaines & Co. v. Turner-Looker Co.*, 1913.

Heritage was labeled "Straight Pennsylvania Whisky"—only "careful observers" would note those differences, and most consumers would be deceived.[33]

However, Gaines might have alleged *too much* when it provided details of its Hermitage label, and in doing so, it gave Turner-Looker a defense. The Hermitage label, it turns out, contained an exaggeration or a dated reference to a bygone method, which came back to haunt Gaines because of the legal doctrine of "unclean hands." Specifically, Gaines stated on its label that Hermitage was manufactured "in the sour mash fire copper way, being singled and doubled in copper stills over open wood fires."[34] Unlike a statement that constitutes subjective or immeasurable puffery, this was an objective and measurable statement. Moreover, at the time, noted the court, many consumers believed that "the open fire process is superior," but Gaines actually performed the first boiling by steam heat, and the second boiling was performed through the use of a closed furnace.[35] These misstatements were not merely "small survivals from a time when they were literally true" but, instead, were material enough to invoke the rule of unclean hands.[36]

Essentially, under the unclean hands doctrine a claimant who has acted wrongly, or in bad faith with regard to the claim, cannot expect equitable relief (like an injunction) from a court. This is the same rationale that guided Chief Judge Taft's decision in *Krauss v. Jos. R. Peebles' Sons Co.* and which guided Barton's defense in *Brown-Forman Corp. v. Barton Inc.*[37] Equity is a matter of fairness, and because

Brown-Forman

Louisville, Kentucky

Old Forester Kentucky Straight Bourbon Whiskey

Age: Unstated

Proof: 86, 90, 95, 100, and 115 proof options available

Cost: $20.00–$55.00, depending on proof

Notes: Often referred to as "Louisville's House Bourbon," Old Forester 86 proof has a special place in bourbon history and local hearts. Flavors include caramel, honey, light fruit sweetness, pecans, leather, and oak for a well-balanced, approachable bourbon that works well neat, on ice, with a splash of water, or in a cocktail. The recent addition of single barrel (90 proof), bottled in bond (100 proof), so-called Prohibition Style (115 proof), and Statesman (95 proof, featured in the 2017 film *Kingsman: The Golden Circle*) make Old Forester one of today's most dynamic brands.

Gaines had not acted fairly, it could not enjoin Turner-Looker's use of an obviously similar brand name.

Historically, bourbon labels and advertising have told all kinds of tall tales and included puffery. Can bottom-shelf brands really call themselves "rare," "finest," or "very old" when they are probably none of those things? Was James E. Pepper 1776 really "born with the Republic" in 1776, long before the Pepper family started distilling in Woodford County, Kentucky? Is it verifiable that Baptist minister Elijah Craig was the "father of bourbon" and the first to use charred oak barrels? Are brands really made pursuant to the same methods and original recipe since the 1800s? These are all examples of legend and puffery that bourbon consumers have come to know and simply let slide past, just like the bombardment of puffery in all other advertising that has become an American tradition.

Puffery Is Part of All Marketing

"Puffery" is not limited to representations that bourbon is "handmade," that a still is "legendary," or that bourbon is "old" or "rare." Instead, puffery is embedded in practically all marketing. Examples include advertising that a portable computer stand is "redesigned and improved," *Interactive Prods. Corp. v. A2Z Mobile Office Solutions, Inc.*, 326 F.3d 687, 699–700 (6th Cir. 2003); that a machine is the "finest" and "most flexible" and "most versatile," *Ellison Educ. Equip., Inc. v. Tekservices, Inc.*, 903 F. Supp. 1350, 1355 (D. Neb. 1995); and that a shaving razor is a "major breakthrough" and provides "the smoothest, most comfortable shave possible," *Gillette Co. v. Wilkinson Sword, Inc.*, No. 89 Civ. 3586, 1989 WL 82453, at *4 (S.D.N.Y. July 6, 1989).

Puffery is even part of the ongoing pizza battles between Kentucky-based Papa John's Pizza and Pizza Hut. In *Pizza Hut, Inc. v. Papa John's Int'l, Inc.*, 227 F.3d 489 (5th Cir. 2000), the court held that the famous slogan "Better Ingredients. Better Pizza" used by Papa John's since 1995, standing alone, was mere puffery. The advertising war between Papa John's and Pizza Hut in the late 1990s was fierce. Papa John's touted its "fresh-pack" sauce made from vine-ripened tomatoes, use of "clear filtered water," and special yeast for its dough versus Pizza Hut's "remanufactured" paste, tap water, and frozen dough, which is reminiscent of early distillers' focus on purity of ingredients and authentic, traditional processes.

SEVEN

Bourbon Leads the Nation to Consumer Protection

L ong before the consumer protection craze that caused obviously hot coffee to now be labeled "HOT," toasters to be labeled to remind us not to use them in the tub, and labels for irons to warn us to not iron clothes while wearing them, product warnings were rare or even nonexistent. Early manufacturers often made false claims about their product attributes or contents. Essentially, there was no legal accountability for making false claims about a product and no protection to assure consumers that they received safe, genuine products. Whiskey was no exception, but it was Kentucky bourbon that led the way to consumer protection. Ultimately, consumers were protected from bad whiskey before they were protected from tainted food, dangerous products, and misleading advertising.

Kentucky bourbon may be less well-known for advancing other noble causes, such as environmental protection and workplace safety, but it influenced the development of those laws too. Environmental protection evolved into a necessary consideration for bourbon producers because the process of converting grain into distilled spirits requires a tremendous amount of grain and, therefore, creates a significant volume of "slop"—the material remaining after fermented mash has been distilled—as a by-product. Although most of the starch is removed from the grains, practically all of the protein, fat, and fiber remain in the slop. Slop from a traditional bourbon mash bill will have a higher fat content because of the corn; hence, slop from early Kentucky distillers became recognized as a valuable source of livestock feed.

However, as America and distilleries continued to grow together, and as the pace of distillation increased with larger stills and the introduction of column stills, the production of slop outstripped the immediate needs of the distiller and sometimes of the local community. Slop was often piped into waterways or sewers, or retention ponds overflowed into waterways, polluting rivers, killing fish, and creating an awful stench. This put bourbon on the front line of conservation and preservation efforts in the early 1900s.

As early as 1904, in addressing slop from the Peacock Distillery in Bourbon County that polluted Stoner Creek, the Court of Appeals of Kentucky ruled that "every person must use his own property and conduct his business with regard to certain rights of his neighbors."[1] Theories of land use rights in the United States had previously stressed the right of landowners to use their land and resources however they saw fit; *Peacock Distillery Co. v. Commonwealth* shows the emerging trend that balanced individual rights with the common good.

Kentucky Peerless Distilling Company, which was recently reborn in Louisville, gave its original home of Henderson, Kentucky, its share of water problems in the early 1900s. As explained in a trio of cases,[2] Kentucky Peerless and its owner, Henry Kraver, were accused of polluting Canoe Creek with distillery slop so severely that "the waters of the creek were thereby made so impure as to render them unfit for use as stock water, cause them to emit foul odors, and so poison the atmosphere surrounding the creek as to endanger the lives of each of the [plaintiffs], his family and stock, make their houses at times uninhabitable, and depreciate the value and use of the real estate along and contiguous to the stream on which each resides."[3] Similar lawsuits were brought against the Eminence Distilling Company in Henry County, where a boy's death was blamed on falling into and accidentally swallowing water from Fox Run Creek, the Commonwealth Distillery in Fayette County, and the Walsh Distillery in Bourbon County.[4]

In addition to environmental concerns, due to their unsafe working conditions, bourbon distilleries also helped the nation recognize a need for workplace safety reform. While mines, railroads, and textile factories rightfully take their place in history as some of the most dangerous places to work, whiskey was not necessarily produced at the bucolic distilleries projected today by many brands and marketers. Distilleries and warehouses were dangerous places, with plenty of opportunities to fall down warehouse shafts, to be crushed by milling equipment, or to be burned in explosions or scalded by boiling hot liquid. Making matters even more dangerous, the distilleries were factories, but they combined the risks of emerging industrial farms and milling operations with the mechanization of "modern" industry. There were plenty of ways to die in these old distilleries.

Lawsuits from the late 1800s and early 1900s paint a vivid picture of distillery working conditions as they describe the inner workings of distilleries and warehouses and then how gruesome accidents occurred. In *Trumbo's Adm'x v. W. A. Gaines & Co.*, for example, a worker stepped through an uncovered hole in a dark warehouse elevator platform at the Old Crow Distillery, where his leg was caught in a thirty-five-inch flywheel and "ground in pieces."[5] The court described in detail the elevator shaft and machinery, how the accident happened, and how "after his injury Trumbo was given large quantities of whisky to drink in order to enable him to endure the pain he was suffering until medical assistance was obtained."[6] The worker soon died from his injuries, but his estate recovered nothing in court.

The Old Crow Distillery's "dry house" was also described in detail because of another injury case, *W. A. Gaines & Co. v. Johnson*.[7] The court described the sixty-foot-long shafting system with pulleys, sprocket wheels, run belts, and chains and how Johnson was caught up in a twelve-inch sprocket wheel that was spinning at one hundred revolutions per minute and was permanently injured.[8] Although the worker won at trial, the court of appeals reversed the decision, telling the trial court to revisit the possibility that Johnson had been negligent himself.[9]

Poorly lit working conditions seem to be a recurrent factor in these early cases. The Pogue Distillery was one of the most popular and prolific distilleries of the time, and it needed to run an overnight shift to keep up with demand. The worker in *Dryden v. H. E. Pogue Distillery Co.* was assigned to the milling room, where "he was put to work by Will Hays [the miller] in raking the meal from what he calls the 'shaker' into rollers, by which it was ground, and which were about five inches below the shaker."[10] The problem was that it was 3:30 a.m. and there were no lights, and Dryden was unfamiliar with this particular job or the danger of the rollers.[11] As might be expected, Dryden's hand was caught and crushed by a grain roller, requiring amputation.[12]

Crushing injuries were just one of many ways to be maimed and scarred while working at a distillery. The J. & J. M. Saffell Distillery operated just south of Frankfort on the Kentucky River. When the distillery superintendent asked a thirteen-year-old boy, who had come to the distillery with friends to pick up loads of slop, to help wash out a vat filled with scalding hot slop, catastrophe could have been expected. He asked the boy to climb to the top of the vat to help guide a hose, and the boy fell in, suffering third-degree burns to his waist and "rendering him a cripple for life."[13]

A worker at the Nelson Distillery Company who was normally assigned to the meal room had been assigned to the mash room on his fateful day. The court in *Kentucky Distilleries & Warehouse Co. v. Schreiber* described the size of the mash room and the mash tub and the precise location and operation of the pipes leading into the mash tub.[14] Specifically, the cold water pipe was turned on by reaching over the mash tub, but the scalding hot water was turned on out of sight in an adjoining room. Schreiber was instructed to open the cold water valve, but as he leaned in to do so, another employee opened the hot water valve, which soaked Schreiber's head, neck, body, and arms, causing severe burns.[15]

Explosions and fires were not uncommon either. In *Kentucky Distilleries & Warehouse Co. v. Johnson* the distillery was operating its bottling line overnight.[16] The foreman called an employee back in after the end of the workday, at 8:00 p.m., to dump ten barrels of bourbon because the holding tank was empty, so that "the

Old Pogue

Maysville, Kentucky

Old Pogue Master's Select Kentucky Straight Bourbon Whiskey

Age: Unstated and varies by batch, but reviewed batch was 12 years

Proof: 91 proof

Cost: $110.00

Notes: Old Pogue is another historic brand being revived by the family, in this case the fifth and sixth generations of the Pogues. Maysville, Kentucky, was once part of Bourbon County, Virginia (before Kentucky's statehood), and is popularly believed to be one of the potential naming sources of bourbon because whiskey barrels shipped down the Ohio River would be stamped with their port of origin—Bourbon County—on their way to the Mississippi River and south to New Orleans. Old Pogue is distilling again, and while its bourbon is over six years old, Master's Select uses older sourced bourbon for the time being. The 2017 Old Pogue Master's Select is wonderfully balanced, with lingering warmth; it's a rich sipping bourbon proofed to drink neat. Describing a bourbon as "smooth" is sometimes frowned upon by enthusiasts, but it is a perfect descriptor for Old Pogue Master's Select.

---

girls" on the bottling line would have work for the night.[17] Noting that federal regulations prohibited the distillery from blending bourbon from different seasons (meaning that the whiskey was bottled in bond), the court explained that the foreman had instructed Johnson to look into the holding tank to ensure that it was empty.[18]

The holding tank was covered with a lid, and the foreman knew that alcohol vapors would collect in the tank and could be ignited by a flame.[19] Johnson, however, had never checked the tank before and did not know about the dangers of using an open flame near the tank.[20] Still, the foreman told Johnson to use his own lantern—which was "an ordinary railroad lantern" with an open flame—when checking the tank.[21] Johnson testified that when he opened the lid and leaned in with his lantern, "it just caught me afire. When the lantern exploded it just flashed out, popped about like a cannon.... I was burned on my face and head; burned my hair all off; and both hands burned, too, there nearly to the elbow."[22] The medical evidence was gruesome. Johnson's burns were so bad that his bones were exposed; the membranes of his nose, mouth, and throat were burned; and his hands were permanently deformed.[23]

Other distillery workers suffered horrific injuries or died in countless ways, such as falling into holes while walking through dark distilleries, for example, when mash tubs were removed for maintenance but no temporary guardrails had been installed; suffering broken bones or "mashed" legs when barrels of whiskey fell down an elevator shaft; getting thrown from roofs while raising equipment on block and tackle; falling down elevator shafts along with full barrels because the ropes used were "old and rotten, and the pulleys out of order"; getting hands caught in grain mills, necessitating amputation; falling down open aisles in warehouses because upper levels often did not have walkways, instead requiring workers to climb on the rick structure itself; being violently dragged up a corn conveyor; and falling down elevator shafts, in the dark, where there were no guardrails around the opening.[24]

While pollution and gruesome injuries helped build a demand for environmental protection and workplace safety reform, consumer protection was bourbon's crowning achievement and an area in which Kentucky straight bourbon whiskey led the charge. In fact, Col. E. H. Taylor Jr. was the driving force behind the nation's first consumer protection law. Whereas Colonel Taylor, members of the Wathen family, and many other Kentucky distillers were making true straight bourbon whiskey, rectifiers, blenders, and charlatans were blending neutral spirits (sometimes including bourbon or other whiskey) with additives and passing off these much cheaper spirits as bourbon.

Blenders and rectifiers could make their product in hours or days, compared to the years of aging required for bourbon. Lower distillation costs, zero barreling and aging costs, and the speed of getting their product to the market gave blenders and rectifiers a tremendous competitive advantage. To make matters worse, no law prevented them from calling their adulterated spirits "bourbon," "whisky," or even "pure."

The real bourbon distillers needed to protect their brands and profits, and the politically acceptable way to accomplish this was to sell it as a consumer protection law. Not all blenders and rectifiers were bad, but there were reports of hazardous additives, and consumers had a right to know what was in their bottles. So, Colonel Taylor—who was himself an extremely well-connected politician—helped push through the Bottled-in-Bond Act of 1897,[25] with the help of then U.S. secretary of the Treasury, John G. Carlisle (a former U.S. congressman and senator from northern Kentucky).

The Bottled-in-Bond Act of 1897 was designed to protect the public, to give assurances about the actual spirits contained in a bottle and to identify the actual distiller of the spirits. Among other requirements the act mandated that any spirit labeled as "bottled in bond" follow these rules:

- It must be "produced at the same distillery by the same distiller";
- Mingling of different products, or even "the same products of different distilling seasons," is prohibited;
- The addition or subtraction of any substance or material, or alteration of the "original condition or character of the product," is prohibited;
- It must be aged in a federally bonded warehouse under federal governmental supervision for at least four years; and
- Producers must affix an engraved tax stamp over the bottle closure and must label all cases, both of which identifying "the proof of the spirits, the registered distillery number, the State and district in which the distillery is located, the real name of the actual bona fide distiller, the year and distilling season, whether spring or fall, of original inspection or entry into bond, and the date of bottling."[26]

The bottled in bond restrictions have been loosened since 1897, but it took over eighty years. In the de-regulation climate of the 1980s, bottled in bond no longer required a tax stamp with the season and year made and bottled, so now brands no longer have to disclose the age of their product. The current restrictions are found in the federal regulations, requiring the contents to be a single type of spirit, produced in the same distilling season by the same distiller at the same distillery, aged at least four years, unaltered (except that filtration and proofing is permitted), proofed with pure water to exactly 100 proof, and labeled with the registered distillery number and either with the real name of the distillery or a trade name.[27]

TASTING NOTES

Heaven Hill

Louisville, Kentucky (distillery)

Jefferson and Nelson Counties, Kentucky (warehouses and bottling)

Henry McKenna Single Barrel Bottled in Bond 10-Year Kentucky Straight Bourbon Whiskey

Age: 10 years

Proof: 100 proof

Cost: $30.00–$40.00

Notes: Heaven Hill produces more bottled in bond bourbon than any other distillery, and Henry McKenna is the only extra-aged bottled in bond single barrel bourbon. As a single barrel bourbon, there will be variations, but they all tend to have buttery sweetness, light caramel, candy corn, and light fruit flavors before moving on to cinnamon red hots and pepper spice. Henry McKenna Bottled in Bond is highly recommended as an under-the-radar bourbon.

Nevertheless, especially in 1897, this law was groundbreaking. As described in *W. A. Gaines & Co. v. Turner-Looker Co.*, a key element of the act was that it prohibited "any mingling of different products," which of course was to differentiate bottled in bond whiskey from rectified whiskey.[28] The House of Representatives draft committee summarized the purpose of the act as providing assurances of purity to consumers: "The obvious purpose of the measure is to allow the distilling of spirits under such circumstances and supervision as will give assurance to all purchasers of the purity of the article purchased, and the machinery devised for accomplishing this makes it apparent that this object will certainly be accomplished."[29] Accordingly, courts allowed bottled in bond whiskey to be labeled and advertised as "pure."[30]

As an added benefit to bourbon distillers, they retained their tax break. "Bonded" whiskey and "bonded warehouses" were nothing new in 1897 because they already existed for purposes of taxation. As explained in *Wathen v. Kentucky Distilleries & Warehouse Co.*, the process addressed storage, shrinkage, and taxation: "When whisky is manufactured, it is at once placed in barrels, and these barrels immediately put in a United States government bonded warehouse, and the government tax on each barrel is computed according to the number of gallons of whisky put into the barrel less the allowance for shrinkage. When the bonded period expires—that is, the period fixed when the whisky must be removed from the warehouse by the owner—he must pay the government tax."[31] The deferment of taxes and the avoidance of taxes for a pre-set, assumed amount of shrinkage were both important incentives for distillers of straight whiskey.

The bonding period and the amount of allowable shrinkage were adjusted over time. In 1880 the bonding period was three years, with 7.5 gallons per barrel allowed for shrinkage.[32] However, distillers bore the risk of leaky barrels or that shrinkage would exceed the tax-free level: "If a barrel of whisky contained when it was put in the warehouse 50 gallons, the owner at the end of three years would only be required to pay tax on 42½ gallons, but he must pay on this quantity, although the barrel might have in it only 30 gallons."[33]

In 1894 the bonding period was extended to a maximum of eight years, and allowable shrinkage was increased to 9 gallons over the first four years only.[34] Understandably, this effectively created a four-year bonding period, which remained the standard in 1897, when the Bottled-in-Bond Act was passed. In 1899 the amount of allowable shrinkage was increased again, this time to 13.5 gallons for the first seven years of the eight-year bonding period.[35] It was a constant challenge for distillers to monitor their aging whiskey and pay only the tax required.

Consumers, of course, benefited tremendously from the act *if* they were willing and able to purchase bourbon that was bottled in bond. Consumers who purchased bottled in bond whiskey received the government's solemn guarantee that the contents of the bottle was exactly as stated on the label and that there were no additives. As explained by the Sixth Circuit Court of Appeals in *W.A. Gaines & Co. v. Turner-Looker Co.*, this was not necessarily a guarantee of quality, but it was a guarantee of the authenticity of the contents.[36] Additionally, bottled in bond producers were allowed to state on labels that the law meant their bourbon's "purity" was guaranteed by the United States government, even though "guarantee" is not 100 percent accurate, thus giving Colonel Taylor and other distillers even more marketing leverage.[37]

Despite the assurances of purity provided by the Bottled-in-Bond Act of 1897, however, price still seemed to drive consumer choice. Even courts noted that straight whiskey was better, but it was also more expensive, which might explain why 50 to 75 percent of the whiskey sold in the United States was blended whiskey.[38] Price continued to rule the day.

In addition to the lower price of blended whiskey driving demand, the Bottled-in-Bond Act of 1897 did nothing to curb production of imitation whiskey, to prevent producers from deceiving consumers with false labels claiming spirits to be "whisky" or "bourbon," or to prevent con artists from fabricating fanciful health claims to promote their brands. Once again, whiskey provided both the villain (the Duffy Malt Whiskey Co.) and the hero (the Pure Food and Drug Act of 1906).

Walter Duffy took over his family's distillery, the Rochester Distilling Company, in the 1870s. By the early 1880s Duffy was advertising his Duffy's Malt Whiskey not only as a tonic that "Makes the Weak Strong" but also as a cure for all sorts of diseases. Consumption,

Can We Trust Food Labels Yet?

Bourbon's role as the impetus for consumer protection laws led to truth-in-advertising laws that are now ingrained in American culture, including mechanisms in place to award damages and to assess fines by regulators and governmental agencies for false advertising. For instance, a class action challenge against Kashi's claim of "All Natural" products, alleging that the products contain synthetic and unnaturally processed ingredients, resulted in a settlement of $3.99 million plus the removal of advertising claiming "All Natural," "100% Natural," or "Nothing Artificial." *Eggnatz v. Kashi Co.*, No. 12-21678-CIV-LENARD/GOODMAN (S.D. Fla., Feb. 1, 2016) Final Judgment of Dismissal. When Splenda used the slogan "Made from Sugar," the Sugar Association sued, seeking $1 billion in damages, alleging that Splenda is nothing more than a "highly processed chemical compound made in a factory," but ultimately settled on undisclosed terms before trial. *Sugar Assoc. v. McNeil Nutritionals*, No. CV 04–1077DSF (C.D. Cal. 2008) Dismissal Order. Separate claims by the maker of Equal and NutraSweet against Splenda, which sought damages for the same slogan, alleging that it misled consumers into believing that Splenda contained sugar, were also settled. *Merisant Co. v. McNeil Nutritionals, LLC*, No. 04–5504 (E.D. Pa.) (summary judgment ruling at 515 F. Supp. 2d 509 [E.D. Pa. 2007]). And in 2010 Dannon's Activia brand of yogurt agreed to pay up to $35 million to consumers in a class action settlement over its claim that its yogurt was "clinically" and "scientifically" proven to have nutritional and digestive benefits. *Gemelas v. Dannon Co., Inc.*, No. 1:08-cv-00236 (N.D. Ohio, Jan. 1, 2010) Amended Stipulation of Settlement.

---

influenza, bronchitis, indigestion, and practically old age itself were claimed to be no match for Duffy's Malt Whiskey. According to false advertising, Duffy's was endorsed by clergymen, doctors, and nurses alike. Duffy bought some of those testimonials, and he falsified others. When one nurse learned that she was featured in one testimonial, she sued for libel (fig. 18).[39]

Nurse and Patients
Praise Duffy's

Mrs. A. Schuman, One of Chicago's Most Capable and Experienced Nurses, Pays an Eloquent Tribute to the Great Invigorating, Life-Giving and Curative Properties of DUFFY'S PURE MALT WHISKEY.

"For that weak, run-down and gone feeling, it is the best tonic and stimulant in the world."

MRS. A. SCHUMAN

"After years of constant use of your Pure Malt Whiskey both by myself and as given to patients in my capacity as nurse, I have no hesitation in recommending it, as the very best tonic and stimulant for all weak and run down conditions. At least twenty-five families use it in my own neighborhood, and when I go out nursing patients ask me what to take for that gone feeling, and once that Duffy's is within their reach it is used always."—Mrs. A. Schuman, 19-4 Mozart St., Chicago, Ill.

Duffy's Pure Malt Whiskey

For more than fifty years Duffy's Pure Malt Whiskey has been prescribed by doctors and used in over two thousand leading hospitals as the purest and most powerful tonic-stimulant, invigorator and health-builder known to the medical science. It is endorsed by the clergy and professional nurses and recommended by all schools of medicine as a positive cure for pneumonia, consumption, grip, dyspepsia, indigestion, nervous prostration, all diseases of the throat and lungs, and every form of stomach trouble, malaria, chills, fever, and all run-down, weakened, diseased conditions of the body, brain, mind and muscle. It is a heart tonic, blood purifier and promoter of health and long life, makes the old hearty and young, and keeps the young vigorous and strong. Duffy's Pure Malt Whiskey contains no fusel oil, and is the only whiskey recognized by the government as medicine.

There is but one Duffy's Pure Malt Whiskey. Insist on having the genuine and refuse cheap substitutes and imitations offered by unscrupulous dealers, which are placed on the market for profit only and which are positively harmful to both body and brain. Look for the trade-mark, the "Old Chemist," on the label, and be sure the seal on the bottle is unbroken. Sold in sealed bottles only; never in bulk.

All reliable druggists and grocers, or direct, $1.00 a bottle. Advice and medical booklet free. Duffy's Malt Whiskey Co., Rochester, N. Y.

FIG. 18. Duffy's Malt Whiskey false advertisement. *Peck v. Tribune Co.*, 1907.

Based upon these false claims, the company grew strong enough to withstand and prosper during the Panic of 1893, and by 1900 Duffy had formed the New York and Kentucky Company, which acquired the George T. Stagg Company and the Kentucky River Distillery (previously, and better, known as the O.F.C. and Carlisle Distilleries) in Frankfort, Kentucky.

While owning these Frankfort distilleries, Duffy continued to market his Duffy's Malt Whiskey for its claimed medicinal benefits. Through the early 1900s the challenge to Duffy's false advertising was building. Samuel Hopkins Adams wrote an exposé of so-called patent medicines—elixirs sold as medical cures but without any actual curative benefit—in 1905 entitled "The Great American Fraud" in *Collier's Weekly*.[40]

While Adams stated that it was "impossible" for him to name all of the patent medicine frauds and that he could "touch on only a few," Duffy's Malt Whiskey was egregious enough that he identified it by name: "Duffy's Malt Whiskey is a fraud, for it pretends to be a medicine and to cure all kinds of lung and throat diseases."[41] Adams acknowledged that "from its very name one would naturally absolve Duffy's Malt Whiskey from fraudulent pretense" because at the time the word *malt* conveyed medicinal qualities, so he was sure to reference a ruling by the Supreme Court of New York that Duffy's Malt Whiskey was *not* a medicine.[42]

A New York court had been considering whether or not Duffy's was a medicine or a whiskey due to certain tax issues, and in *Cullinan ex rel. New York v. Paxson*, it heard expert testimony on that issue.[43] Experts noted the alcoholic content of Duffy's and testified that a "search was made for added medicinal ingredients with negative results." Instead, they concluded that Duffy's "is simply sweetened whiskey." Accordingly, the court declared that Duffy's Malt Whiskey was a liquor, not a medicine.[44]

Adams also refuted some of Duffy's ringing endorsements. Adams uncovered that one of the featured clergymen simply ran a "Get-Married Quick Matrimonial Bureau" and was paid ten dollars for his picture; another was a "Deputy Internal Revenue Collector" and

No Lessons Learned from Duffy

United States history is rife with charlatans and snake oil salesmen, both before and after Walter Duffy. Duffy's transgressions led to passage of the Pure Food and Drug Act and helped foster an atmosphere in which false health claims—while still made today—will lead to legal liability. Popular shoe brand Skechers touted its "Shape-Ups" shoe with the help of Hall of Fame quarterback Joe Montana as a way to "get in shape without setting a foot in a gym," leading to a $40 million settlement in 2012 with the Federal Trade Commission for having made scientifically unfounded claims, some of which were based on an "independent" chiropractor's endorsement, who turned out to be the spouse of a Skechers employee. *Federal Trade Commission v. Skechers U.S.A., Inc.*, No. 1:12-cv-01214 (N.D. Ohio, May 16, 2012) Stipulated Final Judgment and Order for Permanent Injunction and Other Equitable Relief.

Pfizer faced similar problems after it advertised that its Listerine mouthwash was just as effective as flossing in fighting plaque buildup and gingivitis. A manufacturer of dental floss sued for false advertising, and in 2005 the court ruled that Pfizer's implicit representations were false and misleading, also forcing Listerine to pull the offending advertisements. *McNeil-PPC, Inc. v. Pfizer Inc.*, 351 F. Supp. 2d 226 (S.D.N.Y. 2005). These cases continue to show the risks of making unqualified clinical claims, especially with limited or suspect testing, just like Walter Duffy made.

---

racehorse owner, whose actual photograph was not used in the advertisement; and the third clergyman was forced to resign by his congregation after they learned of his endorsement. Adams also discovered that Duffy's employees tricked some physicians into providing testimonials—for example, by misrepresenting that they would not be used in advertising. Ultimately, "The Great American Fraud" helped lead to the passage of the Pure Food and Drug Act in 1906. The act provides that "any article of food, drug, or liquor that is adulterated or misbranded" and transported between the states is illegal and subject to confiscation.[45] The act specifically—and finally—addressed false and misleading statements of any kind on labels and spelled eventual doom for Duffy's.[46]

Other "whisky" producers in the 1800s and early 1900s simply tried to pass their brands as genuine whiskey (without making fanciful health claims), when, in fact, they were selling imitation or "rectified" whiskey. In addition to his instrumental role in passage of the Bottled-in-Bond Act of 1897, Col. E. H. Taylor Jr. also focused his substantial efforts against these blenders, including a prominent Louisville, Kentucky, businessman, another colonel with the same surname: Col. Marion E. Taylor.

E. H. Taylor sued Marion Taylor in Louisville alleging that Marion was misrepresenting his blended whiskey as "straight" bourbon whiskey and that Marion was trying to defraud the public by using a brand name similar to that of E. H. Taylor's bourbon.[47] Marion Taylor formed Wright & Taylor with John J. Wright in 1886, and together they sold Kentucky Taylor, Pride of Louisville, and Cain Spring Whiskey; by 1892 Wright & Taylor had added Fine Old Kentucky Taylor, which became the company's most popular brand. In 1896 Marion Taylor bought and expanded the Old Charter Distillery and brand, which allowed him to distill and sell Old Charter straight bourbon, but he also continued to sell his very popular blended Fine Old Kentucky Taylor brand.[48] The purchase also allowed Marion to call himself a "distiller," which infuriated E. H. Taylor.[49] E. H. Taylor even had Marion's Fine Old Kentucky Taylor tested by a laboratory to prove that it was rectified; the results proved E. H. Taylor was right (fig. 19).[50]

E. H. Taylor's straight bourbon was the similarly named "Old Taylor."[51] He complained that Marion was creating confusion between the "inferior" blended whiskey and the "superior" (and much more expensive) straight bourbon whiskey and sought an injunction against Marion plus $100,000 in damages.[52] After years of fighting in court and dozens of depositions from Boston to San Francisco, the Jefferson County circuit court dismissed E. H. Taylor's claims,

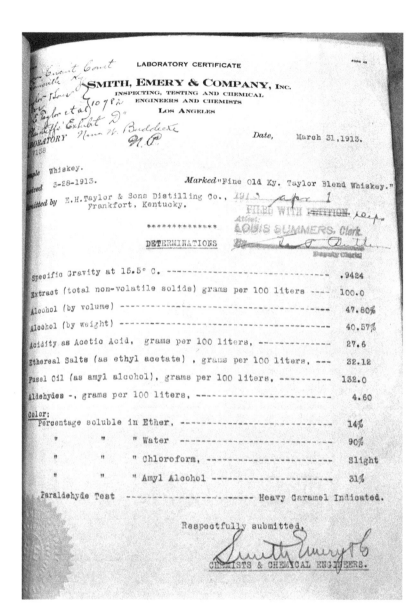

LABORATORY CERTIFICATE   FORM 42

SMITH, EMERY & COMPANY, INC.

INSPECTING, TESTING AND CHEMICAL
ENGINEERS AND CHEMISTS

LOS ANGELES

Date,   March 31, 1913.

Sample   Whiskey.

Received   3-28-1913.   *Marked* "Fine Old Ky. Taylor Blend Whiskey."

Submitted by   E.H.Taylor & Sons Distilling Co.,
Frankfort, Kentucky.

****

DETERMINATIONS

Specific Gravity at 15.5° C. --------------------------------- .9424

Extract (total non-volatile solids) grams per 100 liters ---- 100.0

Alcohol (by volume) -- 47.80%

Alcohol (by weight) -- 40.57%

Acidity as Acetic Acid, grams per 100 liters, -------------- 27.6

Ethereal Salts (as ethyl acetate), grams per 100 liters, --- 32.12

Fusel Oil (as amyl alcohol), grams per 100 liters, ---------- 132.0

Aldehydes -, grams per 100 liters, -------------------------- 4.60

Color:
   Percentage soluble in Ether, ------------------------------ 14%

     "   "   " Water ------------------------------- 90%

     "   "   " Chloroform, --------------------- Slight

     "   "   " Amyl Alcohol --------------------- 31%

   Paraldehyde Test ------------------------ Heavy Caramel Indicated.

Respectfully submitted,

CHEMISTS & CHEMICAL ENGINEERS.

FIG. 19. Smith, Emery & Co., laboratory analysis of Fine Old Kentucky Taylor, March 31, 1913. *E. H. Taylor, Jr. & Sons Co. v. Marion E. Taylor*, 1897. Kentucky State Archives.

finding that Marion Taylor was not infringing on any trademarks nor unfairly competing.[53]

E. H. Taylor appealed to the Kentucky Court of Appeals, and the court ruled partially in his favor by granting an injunction that required Marion Taylor to specify in advertising that Old Kentucky Taylor was a blended whiskey.[54] However, Marion Taylor did not have to pay any damages, and he was still allowed to use his brand name.[55]

While the court's ultimate ruling might seem like only a slap on the wrist, the court was more critical of Marion Taylor in explaining the basis for its ruling. First, the court noted the difference between blended whiskey and straight bourbon: "Rectified or blended whisky is known to the trade as 'single-stamp whisky,' while bonded whisky is known as 'double-stamp goods.' The proof shows that the rectifiers or blenders take a barrel of whisky, and draw off a large part of it, filling it up with water, and then adding spirits or other chemicals to make it proof, and give it age, bead, etc. The proof also shows that from 50 to 75 percent of the whisky sold in the United States now is blended whisky, and that a large part of the trade prefer it to the straight goods. It is a cheaper article, and there is therefore a temptation to simulate the more expensive whisky."[56]

To begin its analysis, the court compared the labels and advertisements used by E. H. Taylor and Marion Taylor (figs. 20 and 21). Additionally, Marion Taylor also used a phrase in its print advertisement that touted the slogan "Drink only the Purest Whisky" (fig. 22).[57] After establishing this distinction and comparing the advertisements used by E. H. Taylor and Marion Taylor, the court concluded that consumers who were unfamiliar with the whiskey trade would think that Marion's Old Kentucky Taylor was a straight whiskey.[58] The court further concluded that Marion Taylor had *intentionally* misled consumers through his advertising by trying to pass off his blended product as E. H. Taylor's straight bourbon, "which had attained a very high reputation as a pure Kentucky distilled whisky."[59]

Marion Taylor's blended whiskey "was a cheaper article, and could be sold at prices at which [E. H. Taylor] could not afford to sell his

FIG. 20. Old Taylor label. *E. H. Taylor, Jr. & Sons Co. v. Marion E. Taylor*, 1905.

whisky," and because his deceptive advertising could confuse consumers, the court ruled that Marion Taylor had to be truthful in his advertising: "[Marion Taylor] may properly sell his brand of 'Old Kentucky Taylor,' provided he so frames his advertisements as to show that it is a blended whisky, but he cannot be allowed to impose upon the public a cheaper article, and thus deprive [E. H. Taylor] of the fruits of its energy and expenditures by selling his blended whisky under labels or advertisements which conceal the true character of the article, for this would destroy the value of the [E. H. Taylor's] trade."[60]

In compliance with the court's ruling, Marion Taylor made clear that his Fine Old Kentucky Taylor was a blended whiskey and distinguished it from his Old Charter brand, which was a straight

FIG. 21. Fine Old Kentucky Taylor label. *E. H. Taylor, Jr. & Sons Co. v. Marion E. Taylor*, 1905.

whiskey. E. H. Taylor continued to pursue Marion Taylor in court, however, including trademark registration litigation in Washington DC. *In re Wright* involved essentially the same dispute, but more particularly, it addressed the appeal of a decision by the commissioner of patents that Wright & Taylor had not interfered with the trademark held by E. H. Taylor, Jr. & Sons.[61]

The Court of Appeals of the District of Columbia agreed that Wright & Taylor used *Kentucky Taylor* and *Old Taylor* deceptively by advertising "pure whisky" when it should have been labeled a blend.[62] Additionally, relying on the Pure Food and Drug Act of 1906, the court noted that Congress sought to suppress "the manufacture and sale of adulterated foods and drugs, and also to prevent their misbranding."[63] The United States attorney general weighed in on the issue too, requiring rectified whisky to be labeled as "imitation": "The definition of 'whisky' as a natural spirit involves as its corollary that there can be such a thing as 'imitation whisky.' If the same process were followed of which we spoke in connection with

FIG. 22. Wright & Taylor advertisement. *E. H. Taylor, Jr. & Sons Co. v. Marion E. Taylor*, 1905.

artificial wine, namely, if ethyl alcohol, either pure or mixed with distilled water, were given, by the addition of harmless coloring and flavoring substances, the appearance and flavor of whisky, it is impossible to find any other name for the product, in conformity with the pure-food law, than 'imitation whisky.'"[64] The court agreed with the attorney general and noted that "blend," "compound," and "imitation" whiskies were all still entitled to be called "whiskies," so long as they contained the appropriate modifier.[65] Therefore, just as the Kentucky Court of Appeals held, Wright & Taylor was entitled to use the word *whisky* so long as *blended* was also used.[66]

However, because Marion Taylor had been using *Kentucky Taylor* and *Old Taylor* at the same time that E. H. Taylor had been using *Old Taylor*, neither of them had the exclusive right to use the name Taylor, even though it could create confusion.[67] The court was clearly disappointed in its own result: "While it is, perhaps, unfortunate that one honestly complying with the law is compelled to suffer at the hands of commercial sharks, there is no relief afforded in this proceeding."[68]

Despite the Bottled-in-Bond Act of 1897, the Pure Food and Drug Act of 1906, and court enforcement to protect consumers against false labeling, rectifying remained big business, and a dispute still raged over what could properly be called "whiskey." Ultimately, the issue rose all the way to the White House, where President William Howard Taft took the reins to define *whiskey* once and for all. On December 27, 1909, President Taft published what became known as the "Taft Decision," declaring "what is whisky," and, remarkably, the distinctions survive today.[69] President Taft reached unassailable commonsense conclusions, such as that producers cannot complain about merely being required to accurately and truthfully label their spirits, whether the spirits are "Straight Bourbon" or "Straight Rye" or whether the spirits are "rectified" or a blend of "neutral spirits."[70] Similarly, whenever straight whiskey is blended with neutral spirits, President Taft declared, it must be disclosed as a blend.[71] President Taft also had to confirm that whiskey is distilled only from grain and never from molasses (which, he clarified, was rum).[72]

President Taft summarized that through his decision "the public will be made to know exactly the kind of whisky they buy and drink": "If they desire straight whisky, then they can secure it by purchasing what is branded 'straight whisky.' If they are willing to drink whisky made of neutral spirits, then they can buy it under a brand showing it; and if they are content with a blend of flavors made by the mixture of straight whisky and whisky made of neutral spirits, the brand of the blend upon the package will enable them to buy and drink that which they desire. This was the intent of the act. It injures no man's lawful business, because it only insists upon the statement of the truth in the label."[73]

Thus, through a century of growing pains, whiskey was finally defined, and consumers were protected from harmful ingredients and false claims of contents. Unfortunately, celebration among producers of straight bourbon whiskey was short-lived, as the rising temperance movement took hold and the next chapter in bourbon history wreaked havoc on the industry.

EIGHT

Bourbon Tells the Behind-the-Scenes
Story of Prohibition

Any discussion of bourbon justice would be incomplete without considering the failed experiment of National Prohibition. Whiskey was seen by the temperance movement as a societal evil, and whiskey is always part of the romanticization of the organized crime that thrived during Prohibition. Despite those distractions, bourbon continued to develop substantive law during Prohibition, including the underpinnings of what Americans see as basic law and order today. The primary stories of Prohibition have already been told; the radical Carrie Nation, the gangster Al Capone, and perhaps most interestingly, the doomed genius "pharmacist, lawyer, [and] bootlegger" George Remus.[1] Bourbon lawsuits tell a story with finer points. The history of American lawsuits follows the building disdain for liquor (including among judges with agendas), reveals how National Prohibition affected interstate commerce, and shows how current-day regulations are influenced by Prohibition period sentiment.

While popular belief may think of Prohibition as the period between January 1920 and December 1933, "local option" laws prohibited the sale of liquor decades earlier. Two of the most interesting bourbon lawsuits that tell the story of these trends involve judicial hostility toward bourbon distillers and the development of laws designed to ensure that defendants receive fair judges and fair trials. As early as 1908, the Wathen family was faced with an unfair judge when family members were indicted for retailing whiskey in quantities less than five gallons, which at the time was the cutoff between wholesaling and retailing.[2]

Richard N. Wathen appears to have been indicted because a group of neighbors near his distillery in Lebanon, Kentucky, asked to buy directly from the distillery.[3] The neighbors were told that they could not be sold less than a barrel, so the neighbors formed a group, collected money among themselves, deposited the full amount for the barrel into a local bank, and brought a bank check to the distillery.[4] When the barrel was rolled out of the warehouse, a distillery employee—at the request of the neighbors and as an accommodation—removed the bung and filled a variety of different-sized containers for the neighbors.[5] One of the neighbors appears to have been a snitch because after he received his gallon, he became the complaining witness who supported the indictment.

Things got worse for Wathen from here. The judge set to hear the case was Livingston Thurman. Judge Thurman and the Wathen family were well acquainted already, dating back to at least 1907, when the city of Lebanon held a local option vote. Judge Thurman supported the local option efforts, and he reportedly "uttered violent and bitter language against persons engaged in the business of selling whisky," promising to use the courts to "see that the town was kept dry."[6] The Wathen family, of course, opposed the local option law, so on the eve of the vote, Judge Thurman made false charges against Richard Wathen and other opponents of local option and had them arrested on the false charge of conspiracy to bribe voters as part of a scheme "for the purpose of intimidating and deterring the opponents of local option."[7]

Judge Thurman refused to step aside for the case against the Wathens, perhaps consistent with his previous statement that in any local option case coming before him he would favor the commonwealth: "I will solve all doubts in such cases in favor of the Commonwealth, and if parties go unwhipped of justice on the charge of violating the local option law in my district, it will be by the verdicts of the juries, and if I were on the jury I would find a way to convict them."[8] The judge was also alleged to have stacked juries with local option supporters,[9] so the outlook for the Wathen family was bleak indeed.

Fortunately, *Wathen, Mueller & Co. v. Commonwealth* helped develop Kentucky law with regard to the removal of biased judges. The court recognized that partial judges "may knife a party that he is trying without it appearing from the record, or without his being able to ascertain the fact," so with the support of affidavits provided by the Wathens, Judge Thurman was forced out of their case.[10]

Rush v. Denhardt is another case in which a biased judge helped define the parameters for when judges should be disqualified.[11] Warren County, Kentucky, was not dry at the time, but county judge Henry H. Denhardt had plans to make it dry. He ran a campaign and was elected promising to rid the county of liquor: "If I am elected county judge—and if I get your help and that of the rest of the temperance Democrats, I will surely win the race—there will be no saloons in Warren county, or in or out of Bowling Green. The people who want whisky will have to ship it if they use it in this county during my term of office. And I will revoke every license now in existence. It is easy for you to see why the whisky ring and their clackers are against me. I courted their opposition and that of every other violator of the law. I have prosecuted them whenever I have been able to secure evidence, and with the power given to the county judge I can put open saloons and the blind-tiger and every other whisky joint out of business as long as I can have the backing of good people."[12]

True to his promise, Judge Denhardt tried to revoke the license of several retail sellers of whiskey.[13] When Judge Denhardt refused to recuse himself and the Warren circuit court judge refused to force Judge Denhardt off the cases, the Kentucky Court of Appeals ruled that "there can be no doubt that the affidavit presented good and sufficient reasons why [Judge Denhardt] should not preside at the trial of these cases."[14]

Other dry counties spelled trouble for distillers too, as overzealous prosecutors searched for ways to punish those in the bourbon trade. In *Wathen v. Commonwealth*, for example, Richard N. Wathen found himself indicted again, this time for allegedly selling bourbon in Knox County, Kentucky, which was dry.[15] Interestingly, the court noted that while Knox County was dry under its local option law, Lebanon was a "wet" territory, meaning that since the 1909 Judge Thurman case, the Wathens had prevailed against the temperance forces in Lebanon.[16]

Also interesting, this lawsuit contains a historical explanation of how bourbon was sold in the early 1900s. Specifically, Wathen employed a traveling salesman who would bring advertising materials to dry counties, blank order forms, return envelopes, and—importantly—sample whiskey.[17] The employee made these sales efforts in Knox County and found four buyers.[18] The customers filled out the blank order forms for two gallons of whiskey, signed the form, enclosed payment, and sent the orders by mail to Wathen in Lebanon, Kentucky.[19] The legal issue was whether the sale was made in Knox County (where it was illegal) or in Marion County (where it was perfectly legal).[20] In an important decision for commercial transactions, the court held that the sale took place in Marion County because that was where the offer was accepted and where the whiskey was delivered to a common carrier.[21] Predictably consistent rules for commercial transactions, and consistent application of those rules, are necessary for modern, thriving markets, and a bourbon lawsuit helped establish those rules.

However helpful temperance era bourbon lawsuits might have been to establishing rules for disqualification of judges and for commercial transactions, support for National Prohibition continued to grow, as war efforts helped the government ease into Prohibition-style regulation. The Food and Fuel Control (Lever) Act of 1917 restricted the use of grains in distilling and brewing, and the following year Congress passed the War-Time Prohibition Act, which banned the use of certain grains for brewing purposes.[22]

It was less of a stretch, then, for Congress to approve the Eighteenth Amendment in 1917 to ban the "manufacture, sale or transportation of intoxicating liquors" throughout the United States and for it to be ratified by three-fourths of the states by January 1919.[23] National Prohibition then went into effect on January 17, 1920. Enforcement of the Eighteenth Amendment was accomplished through the Volstead Act, which provided that no person shall "manufacturer, sell, barter, give away, transport, import, export, deliver, furnish, receive or possess any intoxicating liquors," except as allowed under the act.[24]

Wine for sacramental uses was exempt, and—importantly— consumption of liquor was still legal for those who had wisely stocked up before January 17, 1920, and for those who received a doctor's prescription for whiskey. In fact, every ten days a patient could be prescribed a pint of "medicinal" whiskey, and stories abound about the dramatic increase in "illness" during this period. Six (of ten authorized) medicinal licenses were issued during Prohibition so the demand for medicinal whiskey could be sustained. Licensees included the A. Ph. Stitzel Distillery, the American Medicinal Spirits Company (via Old Overholt), Brown-Forman, Frankfort Distilling Company (acquired by the Paul Jones Company in 1922), Glenmore Distillery, and Schenley Distillers.

While at least these well-connected and lucky six companies could survive, temperance zealots still interfered with the thin sliver of lawful business they had remaining. One lawsuit tested the breadth of the Volstead Act when the sheriff of Dade County, Georgia, seized and tried to destroy a railcar shipment of bourbon originating from the Old Crow Distillery and destined for Los Angeles as "medicinal whisky."[25]

The Brunswig Drug Company lawfully purchased the bourbon from the W. A. Gaines & Company stocks, with all appropriate permits under the Volstead Act, and the bourbon was delivered to the railroad company in Kentucky.[26] While the train happened to be passing through Dade County on its journey to Los Angeles, Sheriff L. M. Holmes stopped the train and confiscated the bourbon, and with the cooperation of the local authorities, he obtained a court order "directing that said whisky be destroyed and poured out by the sheriff of said county of Dade."[27] An emergency lawsuit to save the bourbon challenged the police powers of the state of Georgia and tested the supremacy of the Volstead Act versus Georgia state law.

Warrantless Searches and Exclusion of Evidence

Wathen v. Commonwealth was ahead of its time in protecting Kentuckians against warrantless searches. It wasn't until 1961 that the United States Supreme Court held that evidence obtained by an unreasonable search and seizure—in violation of the Fourth Amendment to the Constitution—should also be excluded in state court prosecutions. *Mapp v. Ohio*, 367 U.S. 643 (1961). This had already been the rule in federal prosecutions since 1914, but the Supreme Court extended the protection to state court prosecutions. The exclusionary rule established in *Wathen v. Commonwealth* is probably one of the most familiar criminal law rules among the general public.

As noted, the Volstead Act specifically permitted the sale of liquor in some circumstances: "Liquor for nonbeverage purposes and wine for sacramental purposes may be manufactured, purchased, sold, bartered, transported, imported, exported, delivered, furnished and possessed, but only as herein provided, and the commissioner may, upon application, issue permits therefor."[28] On the other hand, a Georgia statute allowed the confiscation of "all vehicles and conveyances of every kind and description which are used on any of the public roads or private ways of this state . . . in conveying any liquors or beverages, the sale or possession of which is prohibited by law."[29] This showdown between state and federal authority landed squarely in support of interstate commerce and the continued supply of medicinal whisky; regardless of state prohibition laws, "a shipment of whisky may lawfully pass" in interstate commerce.[30]

Prohibition—along with the Wathen family again—also helped develop the law of illegal searches and seizures, which most Americans now learn about from television police dramas. In yet another *Wathen v. Commonwealth* case, Arthur Wathen challenged his conviction of unlawful possession of a still based upon a warrantless search.[31] The Court of Appeals of Kentucky described the scene:

"The evidence shows that two federal prohibition officers were passing through the farm of appellant when they came upon an old abandoned residence, near a stream, and about 300 yards from the residence occupied by [Wathen], near which old residence they noticed a small amount of a substance resembling still slop flowing from under the floor. The house was locked and the windows covered so that they could not see into the building. Thereupon they broke into the house through a window and discovered therein parts of a moonshine still, some barrels of mash, and other accessories commonly employed in the manufacture of whisky."[32] In a breakthrough for rights of criminal defendants and in line with long-standing American jurisprudence, the court ruled that the federal prohibition officers had no right to break into Wathen's house without a search warrant, so none of the evidence could be used against Wathen at his trial.[33]

When the repeal of National Prohibition finally arrived, on December 5, 1933, with the Twenty-First Amendment, a new era of regulation was introduced, often with remnants of Prohibition.[34] *Age Int'l, Inc. v. Miller* describes some of the remnants of Prohibition surviving past Repeal.[35] In particular, it describes the common "three-tier" regulatory structure in which manufacturers distill (or brew) and package alcoholic beverages, then ship to wholesalers, which then distribute to retail dealers that can then sell directly to consumers.[36] These three tiers are strictly segregated, and in most cases a single entity cannot fill more than one role.[37]

The federal government has also reminded spirits producers that it will keep the reins tight whenever a national interest supports regulation. Just as temperance-inspired regulations were instituted during World War I, for example, World War II brought with it new regulations that prohibited the production of bourbon and mandated the production of alcohol for war purposes. In March 1942 the War Production Board first placed distilleries on a time allocation basis to operate part-time to produce industry-grade alcohol for war purposes, and by October "all distilleries were operated exclusively for the production of alcohol for war purposes."[38] Because this governmental appropriation of private businesses reduced the supply of beverage alcohol, the Office of Price Administration (OPA) fixed the prices of whiskey.

The Emergency Price Control Act of 1942, in turn, brought down a major whiskey merchant of the time.[39] Robert Gould challenged the constitutionality of the act and its application in Kentucky, but he lost in spectacular fashion.[40] Adding salt to his wounds, Gould experienced another aspect of tight *state* regulation, when Kentucky denied him a renewal license because of his federal conviction. In *Alcoholic Beverage Control Board v. Pebbleford Distillers, Inc.*, the court affirmed the Kentucky Alcoholic Beverage Control Board's (ABC) decision to reject a license for a distillery half-owned by Gould because of that earlier conviction.[41]

Regulation was serious, and even today courts still support tight regulation, sometimes based on antiquated arguments. In Kentucky, for example, the United States Court of Appeals for the Sixth Circuit upheld a post–Prohibition era statute that bans grocers and gas stations from selling liquor. In *Maxwell's Pic-Pac, Inc. v. Dehner* the court reversed the local federal district court's decision that had invalidated the statute.[42]

States might be expected to protect their laws from challenges. In this case, however, it appears as if the real source of the effort to save the regulation was a direct competitor of grocers that stood to lose market share if grocers were allowed to sell liquor and wine: a liquor store chain named Liquor Outlet d/b/a the Party Source.[43] The named defendant, Tony Dehner, was the ABC commissioner of Kentucky, and he represented the interests of the commonwealth. Just as ministers and bootleggers enjoyed a conspiracy of convenience in Kentucky in the 1930s (90 of Kentucky's 120 counties outlawed the sale and consumption of alcohol under local option laws), Liquor Outlet allied with ABC to prevent grocers from selling liquor.

The history of pre-Prohibition corruption and depravity, lawlessness during Prohibition, and relative peace under regulation after Repeal all played a significant role in the parties' arguments and in the court's decision and showed how current-day liquor control laws arose out of the remnants of Prohibition. In the 1800s, in Kentucky and elsewhere, "anybody had the right to sell liquors anywhere, to anybody, and at any time."[44] This lack of regulation helped fuel the temperance movement and led to a perception of liquor as a societal evil, so by 1891 Kentucky's constitution allowed its counties to regulate (or even ban) liquor sales.

Liquor Outlet hired an expert witness to testify that before Prohibition "the free market for alcohol" had led to political corruption, prostitution, gambling, crime, poverty, and family destruction.[45] Prohibition created its own problems, though, which were often worse. The district court noted that Prohibition left Kentucky "infested with bootleggers . . . corruption and crime, no revenue, no control, disrespect for law and general demoralization."[46] It was an unmitigated disaster.

Along with the repeal of Prohibition, the Twenty-First Amendment allowed states to regulate the sale of alcoholic beverages. Initially, Kentucky's regulatory framework did not restrict the types of premises that could sell packaged liquor. But in 1938 Kentucky enacted a new statute that in essence still exists today. Kentucky decided on a regulatory structure that required licensure (and limited the number of licenses), *and* it prohibited licenses for "any premises used as or in connection with the operation of any business in which a substantial part of the commercial transaction consists of selling at retail staple groceries or gasoline or lubricating oil."[47] So, grocers and gas stations have been prohibited from selling wine and liquor for over seventy-five years.

A small grocer, Maxwell's Pic-Pac, decided that Kentucky's regulatory structure discriminated against grocers without any reasonable or justifiable basis. Under Kentucky's regulatory framework, for example, a grocery-selling drugstore (like CVS or Walgreens) can sell liquor, but a pharmaceutical-selling grocery store cannot. Similarly, a big-box "party store" can sell grocery items along with liquor, but a grocery store still cannot sell liquor. The district court agreed with the small grocer, and in August 2012 it ruled in favor of Pic-Pac, although it suspended its ruling pending the inevitable appeal.

And of course Kentucky and Liquor Outlet did appeal. The Sixth Circuit Court of Appeals concluded that it is reasonable for Kentucky to choose to prohibit the sale of liquor in certain places, such as those where "the community must come together."[48] Sounding like the old temperance movement activists, Liquor Outlet argued that grocery stores and gas stations posed a greater risk of exposing citizens to alcohol and that more minors work at grocery stores, so they, too, would be exposed to alcohol.[49]

Liquor Outlet (and its expert) also argued that Kentucky must be allowed to use regulations to steer society to lower-alcohol beverages and to reduce exposure of alcohol to impressionable or abstinent citizens and that limiting the types of places that sell alcohol plausibly satisfies that public policy.[50] Still, overly broad alcohol control laws have been struck down previously in Kentucky and in other states. In *Commonwealth of Ky. ABC Bd. v. Burke*, for example, the court invalidated a provision of the Alcohol Beverage Control Act that prohibited women from being bartenders and from drinking at a bar.[51] The Sixth Circuit failed to mention *Burke* and rejected Pic-Pac's challenge.

This regulation is partly just academic since many national chain grocers in Kentucky have separate adjacent liquor stores, so this law is only applicable to small or independent grocers like Pic-Pac. In addition to those small stores, temperance era regulation still has a foothold in restricting unlicensed sales of spirits. While selling alcoholic beverages requires a license under state and federal law, that restriction has not dampened enthusiasm for buying rare bourbon bottles for the sole purpose of reselling for a profit (flipping) or simply selling bottles to friends or fellow fans for consumption. Secondary market sales are alive and well in the bourbon world, despite noteworthy roadblocks put up by online companies eBay and Facebook, both of which have removed sites dedicated to reselling and trading spirits.

The recent dramatic growth in bourbon's secondary market is probably due to a combination of short supply of truly premium bottles, an expansion of "limited edition" and "commemorative"

Buffalo Trace

Frankfort, Kentucky

Pappy Van Winkle Kentucky Straight Bourbon Whiskey

Age: Varies

Proof: Varies

Cost: Varies

Notes: Often considered to be the most sought-after bourbon, the Pappy Van Winkle bourbon line includes Old Rip Van Winkle (10 year, 107 proof, $49.99 MSRP); Van Winkle Special Reserve (12 year, 90.4 proof, $59.99 MSRP); Pappy Van Winkle's Family Reserve 15-Year (107 proof, $79.99 MSRP), Pappy Van Winkle's Family Reserve 20-Year (90.4 proof, $149.99 MSRP); and Pappy Van Winkle's Family Reserve 23-Year (95.6 proof, $249.99 MSRP). Retailers often ignore these suggested prices, however, and secondary market prices run into thousands of dollars, despite evidence of counterfeits and refilled bottles. Each version is now distilled and aged at Buffalo Trace, using the same wheated mash bill as the William Larue Weller brand lineup, is indistinguishable from Weller at the time of barreling, *and is not necessarily better* than Weller 12-Year or William Larue Weller Antique Collection at the time of bottling. While aged longer than most of the Weller brands, the primary tasting notes are similar but with deeper, richer, caramel, luscious cherry, and pronounced oak in the older varieties. Not all Pappy Van Winkle lives up to the hype; some years of some varieties have been disappointing, but that has not dampened the hysteria for this brand.

---

bottles, a perception that quality within certain brands has declined, removal of age statements on many brands and discontinuation of other brands, and—perhaps most important—the exponential rise in popularity of bourbon and other American whiskey. These factors have led enthusiasts to hoard hundreds and sometimes thousands of bottles, and it has created incentives for hobbyist collectors who never plan on drinking the contents of bottles to amass vast inventories for appreciation, trading, and profiteering. Within hours after a new release of Pappy Van Winkle or Willett Family Estate, bottles appear for sale online on Facebook, Craigslist, dedicated sales sites, and countless private sites and forums.

Some retailers (including distillery gift shops) have reacted to the secondary market by raising prices. W. L. Weller 12 Year bourbon, which normally sold for under $30 in past years, is reportedly selling for over $100 at retail in New York City. A retail store in Lawrenceburg, Kentucky, not far from Four Roses and Wild Turkey, was routinely adding $50 to standard brands that have become short in supply. The Willett Distillery gift shop has tested the market with bottles prices up to $750. And these price increases pale in comparison to some secondary market sales.

Being able to increase retail price when demand outstrips supply seems to be quintessentially American and honors the free market system. Similarly, an active secondary market can be more proof of capitalism at work. Just as fans at sporting events detest scalpers because of high prices, "whiskey flippers" get a similarly bad name.

While secondary market sales occur everywhere that bourbon enthusiasts outweigh supply, consumers selling to other consumers are probably breaking the law, although some states—including Kentucky—permit the sale of vintage spirits to licensed retailers.[52] Otherwise, Kentucky law requires a license to sell alcohol: "A person shall not do any act authorized by any kind of license with respect to the manufacture, storage, sale, purchase, transporting, or other traffic in alcoholic beverages unless the person holds or is an agent, servant, or employee of a person who holds the kind of license that authorizes the act."[53] Penalties in Kentucky increase for each offense from a Class B misdemeanor to a Class A misdemeanor to a Class D felony.[54] The legality of secondary market sales may not be a concern where there is lax (or no) enforcement, but consumers should at the very least be concerned about counterfeit whiskey. In June 2017 the secondary market was rocked by reports—and an eventual admission—that an active secondary market seller refilled empty bottles of highly sought-after bourbon with unknown whiskey, doctored a new seal, and sold the phony bourbon for thousands of dollars. "Buyer beware" is a rule of necessity in dark markets.

More than just a "sale" is prohibited in many states. In Kentucky, for instance, the statutory definition provides that the word *sale* "means any transfer, exchange, or barter for consideration, and includes all sales made by any person, whether principal, proprietor, agent, servant, or employee, of any alcoholic beverage."[55] So, at least in Kentucky, *trading* bottles of bourbon could be just as illegal as selling it without a license. Merely *buying* on the secondary market, however, does not appear to be prohibited under the Kentucky statute because buying for personal use does not require a license in the first place.

Similarly, federal law requires a license to sell or transport distilled spirits, wine, and malt beverages whenever it would cross state lines:

Unlawful businesses without permit; application to State agency

In order effectively to regulate interstate and foreign commerce in distilled spirits, wine, and malt beverages, to enforce the twenty-first amendment, and to protect the revenue and enforce the postal laws with respect to distilled spirits, wine, and malt beverages:

(a) It shall be unlawful, except pursuant to a basic permit issued under this subchapter by the Secretary of the Treasury—

(1) to engage in the business of importing into the United States distilled spirits, wine, or malt beverages; or

(2) for any person so engaged to sell, offer or deliver for sale, contract to sell, or ship, in interstate or foreign commerce, directly or indirectly or through an affiliate, distilled spirits, wine, or malt beverages so imported.

(b) It shall be unlawful, except pursuant to a basic permit issued under this subchapter by the Secretary of the Treasury—

(1) to engage in the business of distilling distilled spirits, producing wine, rectifying or blending distilled spirits or wine, or bottling, or warehousing and bottling, distilled spirits; or

(2) for any person so engaged to sell, offer or deliver for sale, contract to sell, or ship, in interstate or foreign commerce, directly or indirectly or through an affiliate, distilled spirits or wine so distilled, produced, rectified, blended, or bottled, or warehoused and bottled.

(c) It shall be unlawful, except pursuant to a basic permit issued under this subchapter by the Secretary of the Treasury—

(1) to engage in the business of purchasing for resale at wholesale distilled spirits, wine, or malt beverages; or

(2) for any person so engaged to receive or to sell, offer or deliver for sale, contract to sell, or ship, in interstate or for-

eign commerce, directly or indirectly or through an affiliate, distilled spirits, wine, or malt beverages so purchased.[56]

Some online sellers, for example on Craigslist, seemingly suspect that their proposed sales are illegal, so they include disclaimers, such as:

The value of the items is in the collectible containers, not its contents.

The container has not been opened and any incidental contents are not intended for consumption.

The item is not available at any retail outlet.

The seller will take all appropriate steps to ensure that the buyer is of lawful age in the buyer's and seller's jurisdiction. In general, this is twenty-one years of age.

Both the buyers and sellers ensure that the sale complies with all applicable laws and regulations.

While inventive, these disclaimers seem unlikely to protect an unlicensed seller from criminal charges. Similarly, some online secondary marketplaces include a long list of disclaimers and other terms of use that indicate that their customers have read and understand this provision of the U.S. Code and agree to by affirming, "I am responsible for obeying all applicable enforcement mechanisms, including, but not limited to federal, state, municipal, and tribal statutes, rules, regulations, ordinances, and judicial decisions, including compliance with all applicable licensing requirements."[57]

These disclaimers and terms have not been tested in courts yet. Until law enforcement agencies clamp down on the secondary market sales or otherwise make it a point of emphasis for enforcement, non-licensed sales will continue. Examples of "crackdowns" on the secondary market are rare enough that they make mainstream news, as happened in Pennsylvania in January 2015, when reports of a successful sting operation on the campus of Duquesne University rippled around the bourbon community. The Pennsylvania State Police Bureau of Liquor Enforcement teamed up with Duquesne University in response to complaints, but they only confiscated the bottle and did not arrest the seller, who could have been charged with a misdemeanor under Pennsylvania law and fined $4 per ounce, or $103, for his bottle of Pappy Van Winkle.

Closer to the heart of Bourbon Country, major news outlets covered the theft of $100,000 worth of bourbon between 2006 and 2013. While it was first reported in 2013, when sixty-five cases of Pappy Van Winkle were stolen in a seemingly inside job, the case developed into a story of intrigue involving bourbon, guns, steroids, bad employees, and thirsty police. Ten people were eventually indicted on racketeering and other charges. The alleged middleman, Dustin "Dusty" Adkins, pleaded guilty in August 2015 to a reduced charge of criminal conspiracy to receive stolen property valued at less than $10,000, which is only a misdemeanor carrying up to one year in jail. One could speculate that these substantially reduced charges also involved an agreement to testify against the final two holdouts at the time, including the alleged ringleader, former twenty-six-year Buffalo Trace employee Gilbert "Toby" Curtsinger. As justice moved slowly, it took another two years before Curtsinger entered his own guilty plea. But in the meantime the case drew national media attention and became known as "Pappygate."

Whatever the scale, it is risky to buy bourbon on the secondary market. Bourbon regulation has come full circle again; Colonel Taylor pushed for regulations to protect consumers from imitation whiskey in the late 1800s, and now again consumers are faced with imitation whiskey in the form of counterfeit bottles on the secondary market. The regulatory answer—this time Kentucky's new vintage distilled spirits law—should help provide assurances to consumers that a bourbon is authentic and genuine while at the same time reducing the allure of the secondary market.

NINE

Bourbon Law Reins in Fake
Distillers and Secret Sourcing

T he proliferation of new bourbon brands over the past decade has included many brands distilled and aged by existing distilleries but sold under new, often historic (or historic-sounding) names. Of course, a truly new brand seeking to capitalize on the bourgeoning bourbon market does not have time to build a distillery, create a recipe, and age the whiskey long enough to make it palatable, let alone for the ten or more years offered by some new brands, so these "merchant bottlers" must purchase bulk whiskey from distilleries or brokers. That reality makes "sourcing" bourbon common today, and it gives bourbon enthusiasts a chance to play detective when the new brands are not being upfront. Many merchant bottlers *are* upfront about sourcing.

Some merchant bottlers have been distilling and releasing younger bourbon and rye whiskies, along with continuing to source the vast majority of their offerings. Other well-known brands that traditionally did not distill their own bourbon, like Diageo and Luxco, Inc., have embarked on massive construction projects in order to distill Kentucky bourbon. In 2014 Diageo broke ground on its own new distillery in Shelby County, Kentucky, the next year it began small-scale distilling at Stitzel-Weller in Louisville, and in March 2017 it opened its new distillery to much fanfare. Until early 2015 Bulleit labels claimed to be a product of the "Bulleit Distilling Company, Lawrenceburg, Kentucky" (popularly believed to have been sourced from Four Roses), whereas now the label simply reflects that Bulleit is "bottled" in Louisville, Kentucky. Similarly, Luxco broke ground in May 2016 on its distillery project in Bardstown, Kentucky—called

Lux Row Distillers. Its forty-three-foot tall Vendome copper column still was installed in March 2017, and by spring 2018 it was operating at full steam. In the meantime new brands using sourced bourbon seem to be announced regularly, with some commanding premium prices despite their unknown provenance.

Bulleit

Shelbyville, Kentucky (distillery and warehouses)
Louisville, Kentucky (warehouses at Stitzel-Weller)

Bulleit Bourbon "Frontier Whiskey" Kentucky Straight Bourbon Whiskey

Age: Unstated

Proof: 90 proof

Cost: $30.00

Notes: British-based spirits giant Diageo has nailed marketing for Bulleit, resulting in one of the fastest-growing brands in the past decade. Using a high-rye recipe (68% corn, 28% rye, and 4% malted barley), Bulleit starts with classic caramel, toffee, and vanilla flavors but then shifts gears with a punch of rye spice, cinnamon, and orange zest, before finishing with slight oak flavors. This makes Bulleit great to enjoy neat but also helps push through mixers to make fantastic cocktails. In 2016 Diageo introduced a Kentucky-only release of barrel-strength Bulleit bourbon weighing in at nearly 120 proof and costing just over $50.00, and the company expanded distribution to additional states in 2017.

Sourcing is not a new practice, however. Litigation between an Ohio wholesaler and the H. E. Pogue Distillery in the early 1900s provides an example of an early sourcing contract. The court in *H. E. Pogue Distillery Co. v. Paxton Bros. Co.* was faced with claims by Pogue that Paxton Brothers had breached its contract to purchase a large quantity of Pogue bourbon, which Paxton had planned to label as its own.[1]

Paxton Brothers was a Cincinnati-based spirits wholesaler.[2] By the late 1800s the company had found success with its Edgewood Whiskey brand, and there was wide recognition of its trademark rotund, tuxedo-and-fez-wearing man, known simply as the "Edgewood Man." Pogue, of course, is one of the more significant historical names in Kentucky bourbon. After suspensions in operations during Prohibition and changes in ownership and closure after World War II, the Pogue family reclaimed the brand in 2003, relaunched with a sourced bourbon in 2004, and is now distilling again. Located in Maysville, Kentucky, near the legendary site where many say bourbon was born—the old Bourbon County, with its port on the Ohio River ready for shipping whiskey to New Orleans—the Pogue distillery was one of the top bourbon distilleries in the late 1800s and early 1900s.

The *Wine and Spirit Bulletin* reported in its April 1, 1906, edition that Pogue had sued Paxton Brothers for thirty thousand dollars because of the alleged breach of contract by Paxton. The district court's 1913 opinion by Judge Andrew McConnell January Cochran (who, like the Pogues, was a Maysville native) recites that Paxton Brothers contracted to purchase 12,500 barrels of bourbon from Pogue, which Pogue was to distill and then age in its warehouse.[3]

These 12,500 barrels were to be labeled not with the Pogue name but, instead, as having been distilled by Paxton Brothers or possibly under its Edgewood trade name.[4] The parties tried to find a way under their contract for bottling the bourbon under the Paxton or Edgewood name, which certainly would have been difficult given the tight government regulations of the time. In fact, federal law at the time would not have allowed the distillery to be operated as the H. E. Pogue Distillery *and* at the same time stamp and label the bottles showing another's name.[5] Recognizing this dilemma, Pogue and Paxton apparently agreed that even though Pogue was in fact going to produce the bourbon and sell it to Paxton, the Pogue distillery would be leased to its namesake, H. E. Pogue, who would operate it as "H. E. Pogue as the Paxton Bros. Company."[6]

This maneuver, they believed, would allow the bourbon to be labeled as having been distilled by Paxton.[7] Judge Cochran found this arrangement to be "the perpetuation of fraud on the public" by representing that Paxton "had made the whisky, which in fact [Pogue] had made."[8] Because of this "fraudulent" purpose, the court held that the contract was void, and it dismissed Pogue's claims.[9]

An even earlier case of secret sourcing was ruled upon by William Howard Taft, Sixth Circuit judge from 1892 to 1900, before his single term as president (1908–12) and eventual service as United States Supreme Court chief justice (1921–30). Whiskey fans most likely know him for his "Taft Decision" in 1909, which clarified the Pure Food and Drug Act and finally answered the question "What is whisky?" by defining "straight," "blended," and "imitation" whiskey.[10] The events described in *Krauss v. Jos. R. Peebles' Sons Co.* all take place after James Pepper went bankrupt in 1877 and lost his father's distillery in Versailles, Kentucky[11]—the famed Old Oscar Pepper Distillery, where Old Crow was born—to Labrot & Graham. They also take place after Pepper unsuccessfully sued Labrot & Graham.[12]

After losing his father's distillery and losing the right to use the Old Oscar Pepper name, James Pepper built a new distillery in Lexington, Kentucky, and eventually he gained great fame. Pepper started distilling there in May 1880 and designed a new shield trademark, which he printed on gold paper for labels (fig. 23).[13] As many new whiskey distillers know, starting a new distillery has high front-end expenses with a long wait before any whiskey is fit to sell. Perhaps to account for this reality, Pepper sold newly filled barrels to the Jos. R. Peebles' Sons Company, a large Cincinnati grocer and liquor dealer, for aging and bottling, and kept other barrels in his own warehouse.[14]

In 1886 Pepper was ready to sell his first run of bourbon, after it had aged for six years. Peebles was also selling (and had been selling) this bourbon under the Old Pepper brand, but after Pepper got into the bottling business, he supplied the gold shield labels to Peebles and other bottlers.[15] Pepper also continued bulk barrel sales to Peebles after 1886, through 1893, when Pepper decided to make Otto Krauss his sole distributor and contracted with Krauss to sell him thirty thousand cases per year, plus one thousand barrels of bourbon and five hundred barrels of rye per year.[16]

FIG. 23. Old Pepper Whiskey label. *Krauss v. Jos. R. Peebles' Sons Co.*, 1893.

Peebles still had a large supply of Old Pepper bourbon, so the company continued to bottle and sell it, using the same labeling it had always used.[17] Krauss took exception and sued Peebles in the spring of 1893, asking for an injunction to prohibit Peebles from labeling its bottles as "Old Pepper," even though Peebles was undisputedly bottling and selling Old Pepper bourbon distilled by James Pepper.

Circuit Judge Taft found some disturbing evidence in the case that might have influenced his famous decision sixteen years later. Evidence was presented showing that, at least since December 1891, James Pepper had been buying bourbon from other distilleries and blending it with his own bourbon—all the while still guaranteeing to the public that it had been distilled by him, as genuine and unadulterated Old Pepper.[18]

The percentages varied each month, but Judge Taft recited the exact percentage of "foreign" whiskey that Pepper had blended into his bottles of Old Pepper on a monthly basis over the course of nineteen months.[19] It was often more than 50 percent foreign whiskey, spiked to 66 percent foreign whiskey in one month, and on average more than 33 percent of every bottle was foreign whiskey over that period.[20] Judge Taft took Pepper and Krauss to task. He recited all of the express guarantees blanketing the Old Pepper label that it was pure and unmixed with other whiskey and that the bottle contained nothing but Old Pepper bourbon distilled at the James E. Pepper Distillery in Lexington, by James Pepper himself.[21] Judge Taft ruled that this was "a false representation, and a fraud upon the purchasing public" and that "the public are entitled to a true statement as to the origin of the whisky, if any statement is made at all."[22]

So, Krauss and Pepper could not stop Peebles from using the Old Pepper trademarks because Krauss and Pepper were themselves engaged in fraud, and this 1893 decision must have influenced President Taft sixteen years later, when he defined the standards for labeling whiskey. In fact, in 1909 President Taft wrote that through his decision "the public will be made to know exactly the kind of whisky they buy and drink."[23]

After Repeal, sourcing was a necessity for many producers that had been squeezed out of business during Prohibition. Then, due to shortages during World War II, increased consolidation in the industry, and a move away from consumer interest in knowing the provenance of their whiskey, sourcing grew even more common-place. In fact, the distillery in Lawrenceburg, Kentucky, now known as Wild Turkey, seems to have distilled almost exclusively for the sourced market. The owner of that distillery at the time, Robert Gould, provided plenty of lawsuits to memorialize his (sometime dubious) role in bourbon history.

TASTING NOTES

Wild Turkey
Lawrenceburg, Kentucky

Russell's Reserve Single Barrel Kentucky Straight Bourbon Whiskey

Age: Unstated (also available in a 10-year age-stated version)

Proof: 110 proof

Cost: $45.00–$55.00

Notes: While the Ripy and Gould names are prominent in Lawrence-burg and at Wild Turkey, there is no more prominent name than Russell. Master Distiller Jimmy Russell—a sixty-year whiskey veteran—is a titan of Kentucky bourbon. Along with his son, Master Distiller Eddie Russell (a mere thirty-year whiskey veteran), they developed perhaps the best expression of Wild Turkey in Russell's Reserve. In many ways Russell's Reserve is a more robust, untamed version of the robust, untamed bourbon that makes Wild Turkey famous. It is creamy, starting with a blast of caramel but moving into a swell of oak, leather, tobacco, and baking spice, with a great lingering finish. Private barrel selections of Russell's Reserve have been some of the best-kept secrets for bourbon enthusiasts.

The property and distillery had been operated before Prohibition by Thomas Ripy and other Ripy family members. The Kentucky Distilleries and Warehouse Company and then Prohibition put a temporary end to the Ripy's rich whiskey history in Anderson County, but in 1933 the family formed Ripy Brothers Distillers, Inc., and began distilling again.[24] On April 1, 1940, Ripy Brothers entered into a sourcing agreement with the behemoth Schenley

Distillers Corporation, under which Ripy Brothers sold to Schenley its 12,897 already aging barrels, along with future production between 1940 and 1944 of another 41,000 barrels.[25] Ripy Brothers became nearly an exclusive contract distiller for Schenley by also agreeing to not produce any other whiskey, except 1,000 barrels per year, so long as the word *Ripy* was never used.[26] Schenley assigned its contract to one of its wholly owned subsidiaries, Bernheim Distilling Company.[27]

World War II and the resultant suspension in whiskey production by the War Production Board as well as price ceilings imposed by the Office of Price Administration (OPA) made "whiskey scarce and buyers were not difficult to find."[28] This scarcity made sourcing all the more important, and fortunes could be made or lost based on the ability to secure barrels of whiskey. Gould was an entrepreneur who saw the shortage developing and who acquired distilleries and barrels wherever he could. He acquired the Ripy Brothers Distillery and its stock, and before that he acquired other stock through the equivalent of foreclosure sales, which did not always go well. In *Gould v. Hiram Walker & Sons, Inc.*, for example, the Pennsylvania Whiskey Distributing Company had failed and its assets had been seized by the New York State Tax Commission in 1940.[29] Those assets included warehouse receipts for 1,861 barrels whiskey held by Hiram Walker & Sons, which Gould won as the highest bidder.[30]

Unfortunately for Gould, who may have still been a novice at the time, the barrels had existing liens and were being sold subject to those liens, as stated clearly in the notice of sale.[31] Nevertheless, in April 1943 the district court ruled that Gould was a bona fide purchaser without notice of the existing liens, entitling him to the 1,861 barrels.[32] The court of appeals disagreed, holding that the burden to investigate and determine the actual nature of any liens at a tax sale should be on Gould, as the purchaser.[33]

Before the court of appeals had issued its ruling in June 1944, however, Gould appears to have been eager to turn a profit on "his" barrels, which resulted in a claim for damages against Gould and a second appeal.[34] The appellate court recognized that "war conditions caused a great imbalance in demand and supply of whiskey, production of which ceased during the war years."[35] Having secured bulk whiskey, Gould was able to have it bottled and took advantage of high prices for bottled whiskey.[36] In the meantime the existing lienholders were unable to buy replacement bulk barrels in the existing market and instead were forced to purchase bottled whiskey at high prices.[37] The court of appeals affirmed the award of damages, requiring Gould to pay the lienholders for the losses incurred in buying replacement bottled whiskey at the then-current even higher prices.[38]

Gould was undeterred, and he continued to buy bulk whiskey in foreclosure sales. In *Gould v. City Bank & Trust Co.* Gould bought warehouse receipts in 1950 for 489 barrels of whiskey issued by the Foust Distilling Company, which had been originally issued to the Sherwood Distilling Company in 1946, then pledged to City Bank & Trust Company in 1949, and then sold by Sherwood to United Distillers of America later that year.[39] Even though Sherwood appears to have sold the same receipts twice, the bank owned a priority interest over Gould because the bank had bought them first.[40]

Whoever ultimately bottled the bourbon that Gould and others chased, they branded it however they pleased, without regard for inconsistencies in sources. The same is true today, with reports and rumors of sourced bourbon brands coming from Kentucky distilleries like Heaven Hill, Four Roses, Wild Turkey, and Brown-Forman. On the other hand, America has made substantial progress since President Taft stated his goal of allowing consumers to know exactly the kind of whiskey they buy and drink; there no longer is any confusion between "straight" and "blended" whiskey. Instead, the current uncertainty is driven by distillation at undisclosed locations and bottling by entities pretending to be distillers and a seemingly limitless array of assumed names. One of the largest sources for merchant bottlers today, though, is not even in Kentucky.

Location, Location, Location

Bourbon consumers have always wanted to know where their whiskey was distilled (often with a preference for particular distilleries in Kentucky), while many merchant bottlers and distillers over the past 150 years have gone to great lengths to conceal the source of their whiskey. At least when the source is provided, it must be accurate, as other businesses are now learning as well. Olive oil shares a source mythology similar to bourbon—with Italian olive oil being the most revered. Amid steady growth over the past 10 years, some producers of olive oil are alleged to have misstated their source so that consumers are misled into believing that a product is *Italian* olive oil. In one case the producer of Filippo Berio Olive Oil agreed, as part of a class action settlement, to make payments to consumers and to not use the phrase *Imported from Italy* except for 100 percent Italian olive oils produced in Italy from olives grown in Italy. *Kumar v. Salov North Am. Corp.*, No. 4:14-CV-02411-YGR (N.D. Cal., Jan. 27, 2017) Order Granting Preliminary Approval of Class Action Settlement.

Similar claims were asserted against the producers of Bertolli and Carapelli brands of olive oil and Safeway, Inc. *Koller v. Deoleo USA, Inc.*, No. 3:14-CV-02400 (N.D. Cal.) (Complaint filed May 23, 2014), and *Kumar v. Safeway Inc.*, No. RG14726707 (Cal. Superior Ct., Alameda County) (Complaint filed May 22, 2014). There will be plenty of lessons for producers of olive oil in historic bourbon cases.

Lawrenceburg, Indiana, is less than one hundred miles away from Louisville, close to the Ohio River across from Kentucky, and near Cincinnati, Ohio. There Kansas-based MGP Ingredients, Inc., operates a large-scale factory distillery once owned by Seagram's, producing neutral spirits, vodka, gin, corn whiskey, rye whiskey, and bourbon whiskey. MGP does not have any regularly released standard brands of its own and instead is one of the primary sources for bourbon and rye whiskey for many merchant bottlers. Some merchant bottlers have been completely transparent about their acquisitions from MGP, but others have not, and the American legal system helped ensure full disclosure. For example, Templeton Rye Spirits LLC, based in Templeton, Iowa, was sued in 2014 and accused of misrepresenting its whiskey as "small batch" and distilled in Iowa, when in reality it was distilled in vast quantities by MGP in Indiana.[41]

In addition to the alleged misrepresentations concerning the size of the batches and the source of the whiskey, Templeton was also accused of misleading consumers through heavy marketing of Prohibition era Chicago gangster nostalgia, including a misrepresentation that the recipe was a "Prohibition-Era Recipe," when in fact it was allegedly one of MGP's standard recipes. The parties settled in July 2015. Under the settlement Templeton agreed to establish a fund of $2.5 million to pay approved class claims and to change its label and marketing by removing the phrases *small batch* and *Prohibition-era recipe* and by disclosing Indiana as the actual state of distillation.

Assumed names might also be used to create an impression that a particular brand of bourbon is made in the backwoods of Kentucky or at least somewhere other than a large-scale factory distillery. Buffalo Trace, for example, is a large factory distillery that, while experimenting with many different mash bills, uses three primary bourbon mash bills: Mash Bill #1 is a low-rye (believed to be about 10% rye) recipe; Mash Bill #2 is a higher-rye (believed to be between 12 and 15% rye) recipe; and the third mash bill uses wheat as the secondary grain. Mash Bill #1 is used for at least six brands (with multiple sub-labels), Mash Bill #2 is used for at least five brands, and the wheated mash bill is used for at least two brands (both with multiple sub-labels). However, the only brand label that admits to being distilled at the Buffalo Trace Distillery is the Buffalo Trace brand. Other brands claim on their respective labels to be distilled at the Old Rip Van Winkle Distillery, for instance, or W. L. Weller and Sons or Blanton Distilling Company. Those places only exist on paper.

Similarly, a picturesque, small distillery in Bardstown, Kentucky, that operated only as a merchant bottler in recent decades—but which began distilling again in 2012—sells some of the most sought-after bourbon that it acquired from undisclosed distilleries, mostly under assumed names. Kentucky Bourbon Distillers, Ltd., d/b/a Willett Distillery, offers Willett Family Estate bourbon and rye whiskies and Willett Pot Still Reserve bourbon but also another six brands (some with several sub-labels), carefully claiming on their respective labels to have been *distilled* in Kentucky and *bottled* by Noah's Mill Distilling Company, for example, or Rowan's Creek Distillery.

Sourcing whiskey and using an assumed name is perfectly legal, of course, so long as the brand does not make a false or misleading representation of fact that is likely to confuse or deceive the general public. Consumers should be able to find the state of distillation on labels, which will not narrow down the possible sources for Kentucky bourbon but allows a solid presumption of MGP whenever the state of distillation is Indiana. And with a little effort and internet access, it is easy enough to search for assumed names in records made available by the Kentucky secretary of state's office. Part of the fun for bourbon enthusiasts is trying to uncover the actual source of whiskies used by merchant bottlers.

TEN

Bourbon Drives Truth in Labeling

F alse labeling—in which fabricated health claims such as those made for Duffy's Malt Whiskey are *not* at issue—does not always evoke the same disdain or rally enough support for passage of landmark federal laws. While this lack of legal pressure allowed many bourbon brands to push the envelope (which itself is another American tradition), bourbon lawsuits still reined in the worst offenders, setting the foundation for today's truth-in-labeling laws. Bourbon law drove American expectations for truth in labeling by forbidding a fake distillery from using a name and images to imitate a famous distillery but showing restraint and faith in consumer intelligence by allowing other imitation where labels made clear that the brands were different. Many bourbon producers learned their lesson to maintain *technical* accuracy on their labels, which is a much-needed skill because today labels are almost entirely dictated by ever-increasing federal labeling regulations.

The earliest bourbon labeling case involved the Mellwood Distillery, which was founded just after the Civil War on what was then the outskirts of Louisville. The distillery is long gone, but historically it is significant because it filed one of the first lawsuits against a competitor who lied on its label about having a distillery (and who also tried to imitate the Mellwood brand). As described in *Mellwood Distilling Co. v. Harper*,[1] the name Mellwood was actually an accident. It was founded by George W. Swearingen (ca. 1837–1901), a Bullitt County, Kentucky, farmer who in 1857, after graduating from Centre College in Danville, ran a small still on his family farm, which he called "Millwood."[2] After the Civil War, Swearingen moved to

Louisville and opened a distillery, intending to name it Millwood after his old farm, on the border of what are now the Clifton and Butchertown neighborhoods.[3] But when he ordered his barrelhead brand, its name was misspelled as *Mellwood*.[4] Swearingen decided to keep it anyway, and in 1895 this brand mistake found permanency when Reservoir Avenue was renamed Mellwood Avenue in honor of the Mellwood Distillery, which had grown to occupy both sides of the street for nearly an entire block.

Swearingen sold his distillery in the late 1800s, and after that it became part of the infamous Kentucky Whiskey Trust (Kentucky Distilleries and Warehouse Co.) in 1899. Having made his fortune, Swearingen stayed out of the distilling business, focusing instead on real estate, as president of the Kentucky Title Company, and banking, as founder of the Union National Bank.

As the Mellwood Distillery continued to experience great success, it attracted an imposter and led to one of the earliest court rulings on false labeling and fake distilleries. The imposter was the Harper-Reynolds Liquor Company, a distributor in Fort Smith, Arkansas. Harper bought blended whiskey and bottled and labeled it as "Mill Wood," used the name Mill Wood Distilling Company, used a picture of an extensive distillery on the label, used *Kentucky* on the label, and included this description on its label: "This celebrated whiskey is made exclusively by the sour mash fire copper process, employed only in the distillation of the finest whiskeys, from carefully selected grain, and bottled only after being matured in barrels for 8 years."[5]

The evidence, however, showed that there was no Mill Wood Distilling Company in Kentucky or elsewhere; that the whiskey was a blend; that it was not handmade, sour mash, or made by the fire copper process; that it was not made from the carefully selected grain; that it was not aged for eight years; and that no such distillery existed as shown in the picture on the label.[6] The court ruled that Harper had used this false label "to mislead the public into the belief that in purchasing the 'Mill Wood' brand of whisky they were purchasing [Mellwood] whisky," and it issued an injunction against Harper.[7]

A different result was reached in 1960, when Brown-Forman's Jack

Daniel's Distillery sued upstart Ezra Brooks for copying its bottle and label design and feel. Due to Brown-Forman's influx of capital and deft marketing of Jack Daniel's in the late 1950s, demand had surged, and Brown-Forman could not keep up with demand. As described in *Jack Daniel Distillery, Inc. v. Hoffman Distilling Co.*, Frank Silverman—another in a long line of bourbon entrepreneurs—created a brand without a distillery in 1957, which he called the "Ezra Brooks Distilling Company."[8] Silverman sourced bourbon from the Hoffman Distilling Company in Lawrenceburg, Kentucky, and other unknown distilleries, and within months he was selling his copycat whiskey to take advantage of the shortage of Jack Daniel's.[9]

It was clear to the court that Silverman "intentionally copied and imitated the appearance of the well-established and attractive Jack Daniel's Black Label package and advertising techniques for its new and unknown brand Ezra Brooks."[10] But Silverman did not stop at trying to make his new brand look similar to Jack Daniel's; he went for all-out imitation.[11] The court described the ways in which Silverman copied Jack Daniel's:[12]

Jack versus Ezra

Jack Daniel's	Ezra Brooks
Square bottle	Square bottle
Black-and-white wraparound label	Black-and-white wraparound label
"90 Proof by Choice"	"90 Proof for Character"
Pictures a small old-time distillery	Pictures a small old-time distillery
"Rare Old Sippin' Whiskey"	"Real Sippin' Whiskey"
"Charcoal Mellowed Drop by Drop"	"Every Sip Is Mellowed 'Cause Every Drop Is Charcoal Filtered"
Small black and white cardboard neckpiece	Small black-and-white cardboard neckpiece
Advertised that it was in short supply (which was true in 1957): "There isn't quite enough to go around."	Advertised that it was in short supply (which was false in 1957): "There just ain't enuf to go around."

Silverman's lack of originality and misrepresentation to the public about the availability of his new brand were not enough to win the

When Imitation Crosses the Line

In-N-Out Burger, the wildly popular burger chain known far beyond its California roots and southwestern U.S. regional footprint, was faced with an imitator in 2007 that used simple red-and-white menu boards featuring a red border and lettering as well as red-and-white interior and exterior color schemes, a "California" tile roof, employee uniforms with red aprons and red visors, and off-menu ordering options such as "Animal Style Double Double with Animal Fries." Only the name—Chadders—was different; literally every other comparison considered by the court was identical to In-N-Out Burger. As might be expected, the court entered a temporary restraining order. *In-N-Out Burgers v. Chadders Restaurant*, No. 2:07-cv-394-TS, 2007 WL 1983813 (D. Utah June 29, 2007).

Another obvious case comes from the East Coast, where a former franchisee of the nation's "most recognizable mobile ice cream vendor"—Mister Softee—started a competing business under the name Master Softee. Mister Softee's trucks have a distinctive appearance, using blue and white horizontal stripes, blue wheels, and the design of an anthropomorphized ice cream cone head with a red bow tie and a blue jacket. *Master* Softee trucks were strikingly similar, using the same color scheme and an anthropomorphized *waffle* cone head with a red bow tie and a blue jacket. These extremely slight differences did not save the former franchisee, and the court entered an injunction. *Mister Softee, Inc. v. Tsirkos*, No. 14 Civ.1975(LTS)(RLE), 2014 WL 2535114 (S.D.N.Y. June 5, 2014).

Ezra Brooks seemingly pushed right up to the line but did not cross it. That's bourbon ingenuity.

---

lawsuit for Jack Daniel's, however. The court ruled that because Silverman used a completely different name for his brand and because the source—Tennessee versus Kentucky—was clearly marked on the labels, Jack Daniel's could not prove that Silverman was unfairly competing or attempting to pass off Ezra Brooks as Jack Daniel's.[13] Hot off this victory, Silverman continued to pretend that Ezra Brooks was in limited supply through advertising campaigns, and that comparison continued for decades, proving that consumers still cannot always trust everything they read on a label.

Even if not all labels can be trusted, reading them closely is important. Bottles today list fictitious distilleries by using assumed names, which might be fine in many circumstances. But some brands pretend that they distilled the contents. One recent example might be Duke bourbon, which claimed on its label to be "Distilled by Duke Spirits, Lawrenceburg, Kentucky." Duke Spirits claimed on its Twitter profile to be "an artisan distiller crafting small batches of superior bourbon." However, Duke Spirits is not located in Kentucky, it is not an assumed name of any Kentucky distillery, and the entity was not registered to do business in Kentucky with the secretary of state.

While claims of being a distiller or having "seven generations" of distilling history are difficult to catch unless a consumer does the research, other label claims can be very informative about what is—or isn't—in the bottle. Does the label use the phrase *distilled by* or *bottled by*? Does it use the vague claim of having been *produced by*? Does it use the name of a distillery that exists on more than paper?

These are not questions only for merchant bottlers or smaller brands; labels from the major distilleries must be scrutinized too. One recent bourbon lawsuit, *Brown-Forman Corp. v. Barton Inc.*, shed light on the source of Woodford Reserve bourbon and taught the owners of the Barton Distillery, in Bardstown, Kentucky, to read Woodford Reserve labels a little more closely.[14] Barton alleged that Woodford Reserve had been touting its three copper pot stills, its cypress vats, its local limestone spring water, and its historic location but that those marketing efforts were false, in violation of the Lanham Act (a federal law that prohibits any "false or misleading description of fact, or false or misleading representations of fact which ... in commercial advertising or promotion, misrepresent the nature, characteristic, [or] qualities ... of goods, services, or commercial activities").[15]

Woodford Reserve

Versailles, Kentucky

Woodford Reserve Distiller's Select Kentucky Straight Bourbon Whiskey

Age: Unstated

Proof: 90.4 proof

Cost: $40.00

Notes: Woodford Reserve is at the front of the pack in fostering the resurgence of bourbon in the mid-1990s and, to Brown-Forman's marketing credit, in helping establish a premium segment. Woodford Reserve has a light nose and has mostly sweet flavors of corn, caramel, vanilla, and light fruit but not a tremendous balance of earthy or oaky flavors, making it best for sipping neat. Thankfully, Brown-Forman encourages innovation and experimentation, so each year Woodford Reserve releases a "Master's Collection" edition that tries something new, either in grains used, methods, or aging. Some editions have been hits, and some have been misses, but the innovation is undeniable.

Barton based its allegations on testimony from a Brown-Forman executive that bourbon sold as "Woodford Reserve" was actually a blend containing *some* bourbon distilled in pot stills at the historic Woodford Reserve Distillery but *mostly* bourbon distilled in a column still at Brown-Forman's distillery in Louisville, using Louisville water, and also aged in Louisville before being relocated to Woodford County for additional aging.[16] Moreover, Barton alleged that until May 2003 every single drop of Woodford Reserve actually originated from Brown-Forman's distillery in Louisville.[17] Basically, Barton alleged that the premium Woodford Reserve brand was really Brown-Forman's entry-level brand, Old Forester, in disguise.

It was true then—and is still true today—that Woodford Reserve and Old Forester share the same mash bill (72% corn, 18% rye, and 10% malted barley) and that Woodford Reserve Distiller's Select contains bourbon distilled both in Versailles and Louisville. Master Distiller Chris Morris has acknowledged this many times.

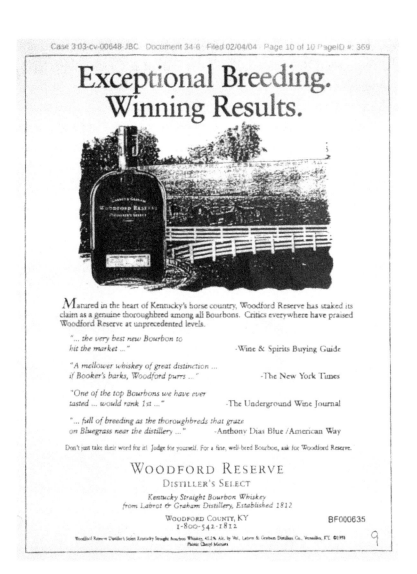

Exceptional Breeding.
Winning Results.

Matured in the heart of Kentucky's horse country, Woodford Reserve has staked its claim as a genuine thoroughbred among all Bourbons. Critics everywhere have praised Woodford Reserve at unprecedented levels.

"... the very best new Bourbon to
hit the market ..."   -Wine & Spirits Buying Guide

"A mellower whiskey of great distinction ...
if Booker's barks, Woodford purrs ..."   -The New York Times

"One of the top Bourbons we have ever
tasted ... would rank 1st ..."   -The Underground Wine Journal

"... full of breeding as the thoroughbreds that graze
on Bluegrass near the distillery ..."   -Anthony Dias Blue /American Way

Don't just take their word for it! Judge for yourself. For a fine, well-bred Bourbon, ask for Woodford Reserve.

WOODFORD RESERVE
DISTILLER'S SELECT

*Kentucky Straight Bourbon Whiskey
from Labrot & Graham Distillery, Established 1812*

WOODFORD COUNTY, KY   BF000635
1-800-542-1812

Woodford Reserve Distiller's Select Kentucky Straight Bourbon Whiskey, 45.2% Alc. by Vol., Labrot & Graham Distillers Co., Versailles, KY. ©1998
Photo: Cheryl Maisuta

FIG. 24. Woodford Reserve advertisement. *Brown-Forman Corp. v. Barton Inc.*

Even though Barton alleged that regular consumers were misled about "the true facts regarding the making of Woodford Reserve,"[18] Brown-Forman had been careful enough to not make any misrepresentations. For instance, the side label on Woodford Reserve at the time disclosed that Woodford Reserve is "distilled for, aged and bottled by Labrot & Graham Distillers Co., Versailles, Kentucky."[19] The "distilled for" disclosure is key. Similarly, advertisements at the time touted not that Woodford Reserve was *distilled* at Labrot & Graham but that it was *matured* at Labrot & Graham (fig. 24).[20] "Matured in the heart of Kentucky's horse county" does not mean that it was distilled there.

Labeling inaccuracies—when they go far enough—can also negate a producer's right to enforce trademark or unfair competition claims. James E. Pepper learned this the hard way after he touted the purity and provenance of his bourbon but was really selling a blend from several different sources.[21] The early juggernaut W. A. Gaines & Company learned this lesson the hard way, too, when it lost a trademark lawsuit despite the obvious deception by the producers of Golden Heritage, because Gaines had been using misleading labels regarding its own bourbon.[22]

TASTING NOTES

Woodford Reserve
Versailles, Kentucky

Woodford Reserve Double Oaked Kentucky Straight Bourbon Whiskey
Age: Unstated
Proof: 90.4 proof
Cost: $50.00
Notes: Double Oaked begins with standard Woodford Reserve bourbon that is matured and ready for bottling, but instead it is dumped and re-barreled into new oak barrels that have first been "deeply toasted" and then "lightly charred." While it ages in these second barrels, the bourbon develops deeper sweet flavors and more oak, for an almost dessert quality.

Outside of the context of trademark disputes and truth-in-labeling regulations, producers still need to comply with a dizzying array of label regulations. The Federal Alcohol Administration Act vests to the secretary of the Treasury the power to regulate bourbon labels to ensure that labels are not deceptive.[23] Federal law also requires a preapproval process for bourbon labels (and all other alcoholic beverages).[24] This label approval process has been delegated to the

Alcohol and Tobacco Tax and Trade Bureau, established in 2002.[25] Without preapproval of a label by a TTB officer—called a "certificate of label approval," or COLA—bourbon cannot be bottled.[26]

To help producers navigate the sheer number and complex web of classification and labeling regulations for all alcoholic beverages, in 2012 the TTB issued *The Beverage Alcohol Manual (BAM); A Practical Guide, Basic Mandatory Labeling Information for DISTILLED SPIRITS*, vol. 2. *BAM* covers substantive issues such as "misleading brand names":

> A name that describes the age, origin, identity or other characteristics of the distilled spirits is prohibited UNLESS the name, whether standing alone or in combination with other printed or graphic material:
> - Accurately describes the distilled spirits AND
> - Conveys no erroneous impression about the distilled spirits
> - OR
> - Is qualified with the word "BRAND."[27]

Note, however, that *BAM* does not address any additional state law requirements and regulations, such as Kentucky's law restricting the use of *Kentucky* to bourbon produced in Kentucky and aged at least one year.[28]

BAM also covers technical specifications, such as type size, legibility, and label placement for required content, such as the specific class identification of the distilled spirit, the alcohol content, and the standard health warning statement.[29] The name of the actual distillery, however, is not expressly required. *BAM* explains that for domestic distilled spirits, the label must include the name(s) and address(es) of the:

> Bottler or Packer or Filler, and/or
>
> Distiller or Blender or Maker or Preparer or Manufacturer or Producer,
>
> "preceded by an appropriate explanatory phrase such as "BOTTLED BY," "DISTILLED BY," "DISTILLED AND BOTTLED BY," etc.[30]

The name can be any trade name used by the distiller, so long as it is identical to the name used on the basic permit.[31] The state of distillation of bourbon and other specified whiskies must be identified only if the whiskey was not distilled in the state already identified on the label under the "name and address" section or if the label is "in any way misleading or deceptive as to the actual State of distillation."[32]

Chapter 7 of *BAM* covers harmless coloring/flavoring/blending materials, using a classically bureaucratic abbreviation of "HCFBM." *BAM* identifies permissible types of these blending materials, including approved coloring materials such as Yellow #5, and provides a very helpful "Use Chart" that covers all classifications of spirits and specifies whether HCFBM may be used and, if so, whether they are limited to a 2.5 percent by volume restriction. The Use Chart shows that any HCFBM is prohibited in bourbon whiskey—straight or not—arguably expanding the regulations, which can be interpreted to only prohibit additives to *straight* bourbon.[33]

This interpretation has real implications in contemporary litigation. Part of Templeton Spirits LLC's defense to the class actions discussed in chapter 9 was that Templeton Rye was not "stock whiskey" because the company added additional flavorings, which caused nearly as much of an uproar as the original claims of misrepresentation. Templeton may have relied on the regulations by adding less than 2.5 percent by volume of flavoring materials in order to avoid having to disclose it, but Templeton seems to have interpreted the regulations to permit the addition of flavoring materials if its whiskey was not labeled "straight rye whiskey." Or the takeaway is that bourbon whiskey and rye whiskey are treated differently, with only bourbon customarily and historically barring additives. Whichever the case, it is an area ripe for more lawsuits.

Age statements are a current hot topic and one that evokes passion among bourbon enthusiasts. During the recent bourbon renaissance, the demand for bourbon has depleted aging stock and has forced producers to abandon age statements as younger whiskies are blended in to keep up with demand. Some distillers were upfront about removing age statements, like Heaven Hill with its popular

Elijah Craig 12 Year, which has become Elijah Craig Small Batch, complete with a bottle and label redesign. Other brands, like Very Old Barton, took another route. Whereas Very Old Barton had been a six-year age-stated bourbon, with a neck label proclaiming "aged 6 years," in 2014 Barton removed the words *aged* and *years*, while the numeral 6 remained. Enthusiasts criticized Sazerac for leaving the numeral 6 but to no avail until 2017, when the neck label was revised to replace the numeral 6 with the proof of the bourbon.

With the importance placed upon age statements by consumers, *BAM* dedicated an entire chapter to it.[34] The regulators clarify that "age is the period during which, after distillation and before bottling, distilled spirits have been stored in oak containers," and that for "bourbon, rye, wheat, malt or rye malt whiskies and straight whiskies, other than corn whiskey (which must be stored in used or uncharred new oak containers), the oak container must be a charred new oak container."[35] In other words, any time spent in a secondary type of barrel for "finishing" cannot be included in the age statement.

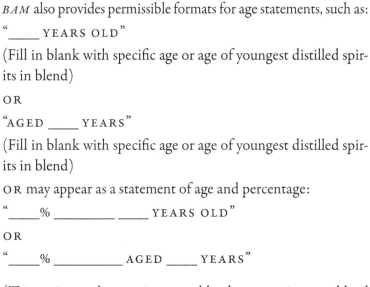

BAM also provides permissible formats for age statements, such as:

"＿＿＿＿ YEARS OLD"

(Fill in blank with specific age or age of youngest distilled spirits in blend)

OR

"AGED ＿＿＿＿ YEARS"

(Fill in blank with specific age or age of youngest distilled spirits in blend)

OR may appear as a statement of age and percentage:

"＿＿＿% ＿＿＿＿＿＿ ＿＿＿ YEARS OLD"

OR

"＿＿＿% ＿＿＿＿＿＿ AGED ＿＿＿ YEARS"

(This option applies to mixtures or blends, e.g., a mixture or blend of two or more rums of different ages. Fill in first blank with the percent of the finished product on a proof gallon basis contributed by each listed distilled spirits [listed percentages must total 100%]; the second blank with the class/type of each distilled spirits; the third blank with the specific age of each distilled spirits) *Example*: Three rums of different ages are blended. Although a statement of age is not required, the bottler elects to label the rum with an age statement that discloses the age of each rum in the blend:

"25% RUM 4 YEARS OLD

35% RUM 5 YEARS OLD

40% RUM 6 YEARS OLD."[36]

Many producers seem to protect blending percentages as trade secrets, and therefore brands that are blended from different ages of bourbon tend to not identify percentages and specific ages of the components. Instead, it is more common for producers to disclose only the age of the youngest component on a label (which is in perfect compliance with the regulation), although marketing materials often still tout the ages of older components. Still, other producers push the envelope or violate *BAM*'s guidance by disclosing ages of components without also identifying respective percentages.

BAM also seemingly recognizes that the use of the word *old* is puffery and provides that if the word *old* (or other word denoting age) is used in a brand name, it is not considered an age reference.[37] Thus, Ancient Age, Very Old Barton, and Old Ezra, while each younger than its name implies, do not run afoul of the age statement regulations.

Overall, federal and state labeling laws not only aim to inform consumers, but they also guard against misleading the public. For instance, 27 C.F.R. § 5.42 provides that spirits labels shall not contain various types of misleading information, such as:

1. False or misleading statements;

2. Disparaging statements about competitors;

3. Obscene or indecent statements (TTB is the arbiter of decency);

4. Misleading statements regarding tests, analyses, or standards— *even if the statements are true*—if the T T B believes that the statements appear likely to mislead a consumer;

5. Misleading statements regarding guarantees (although money-back guarantees are not prohibited);

6. A false connection with any living person of public prominence or organization; or

7. Misleading health-related statements.[38]

Similarly, images that can appear on labels are controlled almost as closely as the words that must or may be used. Producers cannot use governmental flags, seals, or crests or any symbols of the United States armed forces, in order to avoid any implication of governmental endorsement and to avoid any flag desecration disputes.[39] Labels cannot contain *bonded* or *bottled in bond* unless that statement is truthful, and they cannot use *pure* unless that is part of the bona fide name of the bottler or it is a truthful reference to a particular ingredient used.[40] *Double distilled* or *triple distilled* cannot be used unless it is truthful,[41] carrying through the T T B theme that requires truth in labeling.

Like consumer protection laws, labeling laws have their roots in bourbon lawsuits. And like many other American products, bourbon labeling is now governed by a dizzying array of regulations and bureaucratic minefields. Yet despite an overabundance of regulations and official guidance, there is plausible confusion around the edges, so bourbon brands can find inventive ways to avoid being overly constrained by transparency. Throughout history bourbon producers have been known to test the limits.

In the end, though, that is part of bourbon's charm. Bourbon's legends, folklore, and marketing have come to dominate bourbon culture, which is certainly one reason why consumers have fallen back in love with bourbon. On the other hand, tall tales can create a disconnect because another part of bourbon's allure is that it is pure and genuine. These ten chapters have focused on legal stories of historic bourbon distillers fighting for their craft and their very livelihood against rectifiers and charlatans and against each other to protect their own names and intellectual property rights but also uniting for the greater good of consumer protection. Puffery, deception, and infringement seem irreconcilable with this legal history and the authenticity that is guaranteed in every bottle of straight bourbon whiskey.

This contradiction, however, proves the point of *Bourbon Justice*. Just as the American experience is complex and just as the flavors of bourbon are complex, bourbon history embraces that complexity. Bourbon and history are more than just complementary—bourbon law tells the history of America, making it all the more fitting to be honored as "America's Native Spirit."

There is plenty more history that bourbon law can tell, with stories that could resonate with consumers simultaneously thirsty for mavericks and authenticity while they sip their corn. If distillers and consumers realize that lawsuits hold the key—and that those stories can be more fascinating than the myths—then bourbon justice will have proven its case.

ACKNOWLEDGMENTS

After gaining traction through the late 1990s, the first decade of the twenty-first century seemed like a return to the glory days of bourbon. Demand was high, which prompted the development of "premium" brands, and consumers were rediscovering bourbon neat and in long-forgotten cocktails. Surprisingly, demand went from high to skyrocketing, and beginning around 2005, the market has been flooded with seemingly uncountable new "super-premium" brands, which are gobbled up despite astronomical prices, and former reasonably priced standard brands are difficult to find. Bourbon's popularity as a drink has been coupled with an eagerness to learn about its history and its personalities.

My primary acknowledgment, therefore, is to bourbon enthusiasts everywhere. Without the renewed interest in "America's Native Spirit," the historical significance of bourbon law on the development United States would be a footnote, at best, in an obscure textbook. Just as important to an endeavor like this, my parents, along with attorney (and now Muskegon County circuit judge) Tim Hicks, fostered my early love for the law, without which I never would have made the tripartite connection between bourbon, history, and law.

While researching and writing this book—with tremendous help from my wife, Laura, who toiled at the court archives in Frankfort— several bourbon-themed books have been released. One of the best and most thorough books is *Bourbon Empire: The Past and Future of America's Whiskey*, by Reid Mitenbuler. It is a must-read for those interested in the interplay between bourbon and American history. I had the opportunity to discuss some of the remarkable James E.

Pepper and Col. E. H. Taylor Jr. lawsuits with Reid, and those discussions helped inspire me to write this book.

Mike Veach, formerly of the Filson Historical Society and from the early to mid-1990s the North American Archivist for United Distillers, has graciously shared his research and vast knowledge of bourbon history with enthusiasts. He also wrote the definitive history of Kentucky bourbon history, *Kentucky Bourbon Whiskey: An American Heritage*, and has served as an expert witness in bourbon lawsuits. I owe Mike special thanks for his frequent and lively bourbon history discussions and for his helpful comments on an initial draft of my manuscript.

Colin Spoelman and David Haskell of Kings County Distillery in New York—the 2016 Distillery of the Year, according to the American Distilling Institute—also write when they are not distilling from local grain. Their second book, *Dead Distillers: A History of the Upstarts and Outlaws Who Made American Spirits*, provides a fascinating look at the lives and deaths of the people who influenced American whiskey.

Last but certainly not least, I owe a debt of gratitude to Fred Minnick, the influential best-selling author of three recent whiskey books, notably *Whiskey Women: The Untold Story of How Women Saved Bourbon, Scotch, and Irish Whiskey*, and most recently *Bourbon: The Rise, Fall, and Rebirth of an American Whiskey*. Unlike the work of anyone else, Fred's books, articles, and interviews propelled the wave of bourbon enthusiasm to new heights. He also encouraged me while helping me navigate the foreign process of publishing, provided valuable comments on an early draft of my manuscript, and wrote a foreword that would have convinced Carrie Nation herself to give my book a chance.

And a special thanks to Tom and the team at Potomac for believing in *Bourbon Justice*.

On the less formal side, whiskey blogs have been a daily read for me over the past five years. Often addressing "inside baseball" or advanced, in-the-weeds subjects, these bloggers, along with the Twitter bourbon community, help inform the public and effect important changes in the industry, especially those related to transparency. I also learned that the bourbon community is among the most generous of all. The "Bourbon Crusaders," for example, host an annual charity event with a different distillery each year to help people in need across Kentucky and have raised about $800,000 in only a few years. And everyday bourbon enthusiasts are surprisingly quick to share new releases and "dusty" icons alike.

While those books, blogs, and enthusiasts enlightened and inspired me, I might not have developed a passion for bourbon without meeting the people behind the scenes. My first private barrel selection was at Four Roses, and it was the first time that I met master distiller Jim Rutledge. Jim's experience goes back over fifty years to his days at Seagram's, where he started in Research & Development in Louisville, before moving with Seagram's to New York and finally to Lawrenceburg, Kentucky. Jim is the mastermind who finally got the rotgut off the shelves and the real Four Roses available again in the United States, although it took years of his efforts and the demise of Seagram's before it was a reality. Plus, Jim is gracious with his time, meticulous with his art, and proud (without arrogance) of the brand he built. I got to know Jim through many more barrel selections, and he has always been happy to share his deep knowledge, through his Four Roses retirement party in August 2015 and beyond. Since Jim's retirement, Four Roses has continued to fire on all cylinders with new master distiller Brent Elliott.

The visionaries behind Peristyle LLC—Will Arvin and Wes Murry—continue to inspire the bourbon community with progress at the historic landmark Old Taylor Distillery in Millville, Kentucky, where they resurrected the Old Taylor Distillery as Castle & Key Distillery and began distilling in 2017. And although she was only there briefly, Kentucky's first female master distiller since Prohibition, Marianne Eaves, has been generous with her time with me and in our discussions about recipes and barrel-entry proof.

Chris Morris of Brown-Forman / Woodford Reserve made time for me for dinner at a Louisville bourbon destination—Bourbon's Bistro—and shared the results of his archaeological investigation at the Old Oscar Pepper property and the litigation between James

Pepper and his own mother over control of the distillery. The care taken by Brown-Forman in the mid-1990s to reestablish the Labrot & Graham Old Oscar Pepper Distillery as a premiere distillery foreshadowed bourbon's resurgence, and Brown-Forman continues to treat that history with deserved respect.

Bill Samuels Jr. is one of the many gregarious entertainers of the group. He can regale a crowd with stories about his father setting off on his own, his mother developing the perfect red wax in her kitchen, and getting started with a yeast strain from (*gasp*) Pappy Van Winkle himself—not always the official yeast story from Maker's Mark. With some people affability and charm cover a lack of substance but not so with Bill. A crab and crawfish boil hosted by Bill and his wife, Nancy, as part of a bourbon fantasy camp called the "Kentucky Bourbon Affair" proved to be my perfect opportunity to dive into some substantive Maker's Mark details with Bill, like aging (and barrel rotation), entry proof, his take on cask strength bottling, consumer impressions, and upcoming releases.

There are many, *many* more inspirational people beyond the master distillers and primary spokespeople. Brand ambassadors like Bernie Lubbers and the late Al Young, tour guides like Freddie Johnson, passionate distillers like Lisa Wicker, and brothers reigniting a family legacy like Steve and Paul Beam round out company that we all want to keep. Bourbon and its people are quintessential Americana.

1. Bourbon History Tells the Story

1. S. Con. Res. 19, 88th Cong., 78 Stat. 1208 (May 4, 1964).

2. The so-called Whiskey Tax, ch. 15, 1 Stat. 199 (March 3, 1791), was adopted in order to fund the national debt incurred during the Revolutionary War.

3. Newcomb-Buchanan Co. v. Baskett, 14 Bush 658, 77 Ky. 658, 661 (1879).

4. *See, e.g.,* United States v. 50 Barrels of Whisky, 165 F. 966, 968 (D. Md. 1908).

5. E. H. Taylor, Jr. & Sons Co. v. Marion E. Taylor, 27 Ky. L. Rptr., 124 Ky. 173, 85 S.W. 1085, 1086 (1905).

6. Bottled-in-Bond Act of 1897, ch. 379, 29 Stat. 626 (1897).

7. *See, e.g.,* National Distillers Products Corp. v. K. Taylor Distilling Co., 31 F. Supp. 611 (E.D. Ky. 1940) (where post-Repeal entrepreneurs used the well-established Taylor name), as discussed in ch. 5.

8. Churchill Downs Distilling Co. v. Churchill Downs, Inc., 262 Ky. 567, 90 S.W.2d 1041 (1936); *see* ch. 5.

9. Country Distillers Products, Inc. v. Samuels, Inc., 309 Ky. 262, 217 S.W.2d 216 (1948); *see* ch. 3.

10. Mellwood Distilling Co. v. Harper, 167 F. 389, 392 (W.D. Ark. 1908); *see* ch. 10.

11. Maker's Mark Distillery, Inc. v. Diageo North Am., Inc., 679 F.3d 410 (6th Cir. 2012).

12. Salters v. Beam Suntory, Inc., Case No. 4:14cv659-RH/CAS, 2015 WL 2124939 (N.D. Fla. May 1, 2015).

2. American Law Defines Bourbon

1. Even the spelling makes a difference—maybe. The spelling of *whisky* versus *whiskey* is typically attributed to a distinction between Scottish (without the *e*) and the American versions (with the *e*), but as seen in statutes and lawsuits through the mid-twentieth century, American courts used the Scottish spelling. In fact, *current* federal statutes still use the Scottish spelling, as does Maker's Mark, one of the world's most recognizable brands of "Kentucky Straight Bourbon Whisky." On the other hand, almost every other brand of American whiskey uses the *-ey* spelling, so the best advice may be to use *whiskey* when referring to American spirits distilled from grain but to accept the *whisky* spelling without being overly dogmatic. *See also* Maker's Mark Distillery, Inc. v. Diageo North Am., Inc., 679 F.3d 410, 414, n.1 (6th Cir. 2012).

2. 27 C.F.R. § 5.22(b).

3. *See* 27 C.F.R. § 5.22(b)(1)(i).

4. 27 C.F.R. § 5.22(l)(1).

5. *See, e.g.*, North American Free Trade Agreement, U.S.-Can.-Mex., Dec. 17, 1992, 32 I.L.M. 289, 319 (1993) ("Canada and Mexico shall recognize Bourbon Whiskey ... as [a] distinctive product[s] of the United States. Accordingly, Canada and Mexico shall not permit the sale of any product as Bourbon Whiskey unless it has been manufactured in the United States in accordance with the laws and regulations of the United States governing the manufacture of Bourbon Whiskey"); Council Regulation 1267/94, 1994 O.J. (L 138) 1 (EC); United States–Australia Free Trade Agreement, U.S.-Austl., May 18, 2004, Side Letter, Distinctive Products ("Australia shall not permit the sale of any product as Bourbon Whiskey ... unless it has been manufactured in the United States according to the laws of the United States governing the manufacture of Bourbon Whiskey and complies with all applicable U.S. regulations for the consumption, sale, or export as Bourbon Whiskey").

6. Rare Breed Distilling v. Heaven Hill Distilleries, No. C-09-04728 EDL, 2010 WL 335658, *1 (N.D. Cal. Jan. 22, 2010).

7. United States v. 50 Barrels of Whisky, 165 F. 966, 967 (D. Md. 1908).

8. *See, e.g.*, Levy v. Uri, 31 App. D.C. 441, 445 (D.C. Cir. 1908) ("It is well understood that bourbon whiskey is a Kentucky product made principally out of corn, with sufficient rye and barley malt added to distinguish it from straight corn whiskey"); W. A. Gaines & Co. v. Rock Spring Distilling Co., 226 F. 531, 539 n.3 (6th Cir. 1915) ("Assuming that, at that date [1870], 'Bourbon' fairly meant a corn whisky from somewhere in Kentucky, even if not from Bourbon county").

9. Niels Christian Ortved, "The Making of Fine Kentucky Whisky," *Wine and Spirit Bulletin*, 19, no. 5, May 1, 1905, 20.

10. *See, e.g.*, In re Majestic Distilling Co., 420 F.2d 1086, 1087 (C.C.P.A. 1970) (citing *Webster's Third International Dictionary* [1966] for its definition of *bourbon whiskey* as "a whiskey distilled from a mash containing at least 51 percent corn, the rest being malt and rye, and aged in new charred oak containers").

11. Brown-Forman Corp. v. Merrick, No. 2014-SC-000717-DG, 2017 WL 4296968, *1 (Ky. Sept. 28, 2017) ("Before being labeled bourbon, the distilled spirit must be aged a minimum of two-years in new charred-oak barrels" [citing 27 C.F.R. § 5.22]).

12. 27 C.F.R. § 5.22(b)(1)(iii).

13. 27 C.F.R. § 5.11.

14. 27 C.F.R. § 5.40(a).

15. 27 C.F.R. § 5.40(a)(1), (e)(1), (e)(2).

16. 27 C.F.R. § 5.40(a)(1), (e)(1), (e)(2).

17. *See The Beverage Alcohol Manual (BAM): A Practical Guide, Basic Mandatory Labeling Information for DISTILLED SPIRITS*, vol. 2 (Washington DC: Department of the Treasury, 2012), ch. 7, 10 (disallowing harmless coloring/flavoring/blending materials for "Whisky [Bourbon]").

18. 27 C.F.R. § 5.23(a)(2).

19. E. H. Taylor, Jr. & Sons Co. v. Marion E. Taylor, 27 Ky. L. Rptr., 124 Ky. 173, 85 S.W. 1085, 1086 (1905).

20. Ch. 3915, 34 Stat. 768 (1906).

21. United States v. 50 Barrels of Whisky, 165 F. 966, 970 (D. Md. 1908).

22. *50 Barrels of Whisky*, 165 F. at 970.

23. *Krauss v. Jos. R. Peebles' Sons Co.*, 58 F. 585, 593–94 (S.D. Ohio 1893).

24. Maker's Mark Distillery, Inc. v. Diageo North Am., Inc., 679 F.3d 410, 416 (6th Cir. 2012), citing H. Parker Willis, "What Whiskey Is," *McClure's Magazine* 34 (1910): 687, 699.

25. *Maker's Mark*, 679 F.3d at 416.

26. *Maker's Mark*, 679 F.3d at 416.

27. *Maker's Mark*, 679 F.3d at 416.

28. 27 C.F.R. § 5.22(b)(1)(iii); 27 C.F.R. § 5.23(a)(2).

29. W. A. Gaines & Co. v. Rock Spring Distilling Co., 226 F. 531, 545 (6th Cir. 1915).

30. Ky. Rev. Stat. Ann. § 244.370.

31. Levy v. Uri, 31 App. D.C. 441, 445 (D.C. Cir. 1908).

32. 27 C.F.R. § 5.22(b)(1)(i). *See also* Federal Bureau of Alcohol, Tobacco, and Firearms Ruling 79-9 (1979).

33. Salters v. Beam Suntory, Inc., Case No. 4:14cv659-RH/CAS, 2015 WL 2124939 (N.D. Fla. May 1, 2015); Nowrouzi v. Maker's Mark Distillery, Inc., Civil No. 14cv2885 JAH (NLS), 2015 WL 4523551 (S.D. Cal. July 27, 2015).

34. S. Con. Res. 19, 88th Cong., 78 Stat. 1208 (May 4, 1964).

3. Development of Trademark, Name Rights

1. Kentucky Distilleries & Warehouse Co. v. Wathen, 110 F. 641, 642–43 (C.C. W.D. Ky. 1901) (citing Sec. 3295, Rev. Stat., as amended by the act of July 16, 1892, 27 Stat. 201).

2. Labrot & Graham's Old Oscar Pepper Distillery National Historic Landmark Application, 4.

3. Labrot & Graham's National Historic Landmark Application, *supra*, at 34.

4. Labrot & Graham's National Historic Landmark Application, *supra*, at 46.

5. Labrot & Graham's National Historic Landmark Application, *supra*, at 8.

6. Labrot & Graham's National Historic Landmark Application, *supra*, at 9.

7. Labrot & Graham's National Historic Landmark Application, *supra*, at 9, 24, 31–32.

8. Labrot & Graham's National Historic Landmark Application, *supra*, at 31, 39.

9. Labrot & Graham's National Historic Landmark Application, *supra*, at 36.

10. Labrot & Graham's National Historic Landmark Application, *supra*, at 38.

11. Labrot & Graham's National Historic Landmark Application, *supra*, at 38–39.

12. Labrot & Graham's National Historic Landmark Application, *supra*, at 39.

13. Pepper v. Labrot, 8 F. 29 (C.C.D. Ky. 1881).

14. *Pepper*, 8 F. at 38.

15. *Pepper*, 8 F. at 33–34, 38–39.

16. *Pepper*, 8 F. at 38.

17. Newcomb-Buchannan Co. v. Baskett, 14 Bush 658, 77 Ky. 658, 662 (1879).

18. Geo. T. Stagg Co. v. Taylor, 16 Ky. L. Rptr. 213, 95 Ky. 651, 27 S.W. 247, 248 (1894).

19. *Pepper*, 8 F. at 39.

20. *Pepper*, 8 F. at 34.

21. *Pepper*, 8 F. at 34.

22. *Pepper*, 8 F. at 31–32.

23. *Pepper*, 8 F. at 30.

24. *Pepper*, 8 F. at 37.

25. *Pepper*, 8 F. at 30.

26. *Pepper*, 8 F. at 31.

27. *Pepper*, 8 F. at 38.

28. *Pepper*, 8 F. at 38.

29. *Pepper*, 8 F. at 38.

30. *Pepper*, 8 F. at 31.

31. *Pepper*, 8 F. at 32.

32. *Pepper*, 8 F. at 39.

33. *Pepper*, 8 F. at 39.

34. *Pepper*, 8 F. at 41.

35. *Pepper*, 8 F. at 41.

36. Newcomb-Buchannan Co. v. Baskett, 14 Bush 658, 77 Ky. 658 (1879).

37. *Newcomb-Buchanan Co.*, 77 Ky. at 661.

38. *Newcomb-Buchanan Co.*, 77 Ky. at 661.

39. *Newcomb-Buchanan Co.*, 77 Ky. at 661.

40. *Newcomb-Buchanan Co.*, 77 Ky. at 661–62.

41. *Newcomb-Buchanan Co.*, 77 Ky. at 662.

42. Newcomb-Buchannan Co. v. Baskett, Oldham Circuit Court, Civil Order Book, May 12, 1879.

43. *Newcomb-Buchanan Co.*, 77 Ky. at 666. Newcomb-Buchanan appealed a second time after the trial court awarded damages, arguing this time that Baskett had authorized Colonel Taylor to resell the 150 barrels at issue. This argument was rejected too. Newcomb-Buchanan Co. v. Baskett, 4 Ky. L. Rptr. 828 (1883).

44. Geo. T. Stagg Co. v. Taylor, 16 Ky. L. Rptr. 213, 95 Ky. 651, 27 S.W. 247, 248 (1894).

45. *Geo. T. Stagg Co.*, 27 S.W. at 248.

46. *Geo. T. Stagg Co.*, 27 S.W. at 248.

47. *Geo. T. Stagg Co.*, 27 S.W. at 249.

48. *Geo. T. Stagg Co.*, 27 S.W. at 248–49.

49. *Geo. T. Stagg Co.*, 27 S.W. at 249. *See also* E. H. Taylor Jr. & Sons v. Geo. T. Stagg Co., Franklin Circuit Court, Mar. 12, 1900, dep. of George H. Watson (the bookkeeper for the E. H. Taylor, Jr. Co. and president of the company after Colonel Taylor severed his connection with Stagg), at 2, 9.

50. *Geo. T. Stagg Co.*, 27 S.W. at 248–49.

51. *Geo. T. Stagg Co.*, 27 S.W. at 249.

52. *Geo. T. Stagg Co.*, 27 S.W. at 249.

53. *Geo. T. Stagg Co.*, 27 S.W. at 249.

54. *Geo. T. Stagg Co.*, 27 S.W. at 250.

55. *Geo. T. Stagg Co.*, 27 S.W. at 250.

56. *Geo. T. Stagg Co.*, 27 S.W. at 250. J. Swigert Taylor followed his father's footsteps into distilling and had acquired the distillery in 1880. He sold it to the company bearing his father's name but controlled by Stagg in 1882, although he continued to operate the distillery. *See* E. H. Taylor Jr. v. Marion E. Taylor, No. 10782, Jefferson Circuit Court, Apr. 14, 1898, dep. of J. Swigert Taylor, 2. Colonel Taylor had an even earlier connection with the distillery according to Swigert's testimony: while associated with W. A. Gaines & Co. in the 1860s, he made Old Crow there. Apr. 14, 1898, dep. of J. Swigert Taylor, at 4.

57. *Geo. T. Stagg Co.*, 27 S.W. at 250.

58. *Geo. T. Stagg Co.*, 27 S.W. at 250. *See also* E. H. Taylor Jr. & Sons v. Geo. T. Stagg Co., Franklin Circuit Court, Mar. 9, 1898 dep. of Colonel Taylor, 37.

59. *Geo. T. Stagg Co.*, 27 S.W. at 250.

60. *Geo. T. Stagg Co.*, 27 S.W. at 250–51.

61. *Geo. T. Stagg Co.*, 27 S.W. at 251.

62. *Geo. T. Stagg Co.*, 27 S.W. at 248.

63. *E. H. Taylor Jr. & Sons,* (Franklin Circuit Court), Apr. 9, 1891, Order, at 1–2.

64. E. H. Taylor Jr. & Sons, (Franklin Circuit Court), Apr. 9, 1891, Order, at 8.

65. *Geo. T. Stagg Co.*, 27 S.W. at 251.

66. *Geo. T. Stagg Co.*, 27 S.W. at 249.

67. *E. H. Taylor Jr. & Sons,* (Franklin Circuit Court) Exhibit A.

68. *Geo. T. Stagg Co.*, 27 S.W. at 249.

69. *Geo. T. Stagg Co.*, 27 S.W. at 259.

70. *Geo. T. Stagg Co.*, 27 S.W. at 251.

71. Taylor v. Geo. T. Stagg Co., 18 Ky. L. Rptr. 680, 37 S.W. 954 (1896).

72. *Taylor*, 37 S.W. at 954.

73. *Taylor*, 37 S.W. at 955.

74. Geo. T. Stagg Co. v. E. H. Taylor & Sons, 24 Ky. L. Rptr. 495, 113 Ky. 709, 68 S.W. 862 (1902).

75. Stagg died while the case was pending, and the notorious Walter P. Duffy (see ch. 7) became the owner of the O.F.C. and Carlisle through the New York and Kentucky Company, which gave Colonel Taylor all the more reason to distance himself from the O.F.C. and to protect his name from misappropriation. *E. H. Taylor Jr. & Sons* (Franklin Circuit Court), Apr. 6, 1900, dep. of J. Swigert Taylor, at 1–2.

76. *Geo. T. Stagg Co.*, 68 S.W. at 867.

77. Maker's Mark Distillery, Inc. v. Diageo North Am., Inc., 703 F. Supp. 2d 671, 680–81 (W.D. Ky. 2010).

78. *Maker's Mark*, 703 F. Supp. 2d at 681.

79. *Maker's Mark*, 703 F. Supp. 2d at 681.

80. *Maker's Mark*, 703 F. Supp. 2d at 681.

81. *Maker's Mark*, 703 F. Supp. 2d at 682.

82. *Maker's Mark*, 703 F. Supp. 2d at 682.

83. *Maker's Mark*, 703 F. Supp. 2d at 682.

84. *Maker's Mark*, 703 F. Supp. 2d at 704.

85. Maker's Mark Distillery, Inc. v. Diageo North Am., Inc., 679 F.3d 410 (6th Cir. 2012).

86. Maker's Mark Distillery, Inc. v. Diageo North Am., Inc., Appellants' Brief, 2010 WL 6544937 *5, 37 (6th Cir. Sept. 17, 2010).

87. *Maker's Mark*, Appellants' Brief, 2010 wl 6544937, at *21.

88. *Maker's Mark*, Appellants' Brief, 2010 wl 6544937, at *21.

89. *Maker's Mark*, Appellants' Brief, 2010 wl 6544937, at *21.

90. *Maker's Mark*, Appellants' Brief, 2010 wl 6544937, at *22.

91. *Maker's Mark*, Appellants' Brief, 2010 wl 6544937, at *23.

92. *Maker's Mark*, 679 F.3d at 414.

93. *Maker's Mark*, 679 F.3d at 414–17 (citing David P. Garion, "Maker's Mark Goes Against the Grain to Make Its Mark," *Wall Street Journal*, Aug. 1, 1980, 1). Practically a fluke, David Garion was at the Brown Hotel Bar in Louisville, after covering a Humana Corp. annual meeting, when he struck up a conversation with a bartender who knew Bill Samuels Jr. Bill Jr. tricked his father into meeting Garion the next morning, resulting in one of Bill Sr.'s three interviews ever granted. By 8:15 a.m. on August 1, Maker's Mark had to order five new phone lines. Then Bill Sr. and Bill Jr. personally responded to the over twenty-five thousand letters they received as a result of the article. The rest is history.

94. *Maker's Mark*, 679 F.3d at 417.

95. *Maker's Mark*, 679 F.3d at 424–25.

96. *Maker's Mark*, 703 F. Supp. 2d at 705.

4. Most Comprehensive Trade Name Case Study

1. *See* E. H. Taylor Jr. v. Marion E. Taylor, No. 10782, Jefferson Circuit Court, June 14, 1902 dep. of S.C. Herbst, 5.

2. The demise of Old Crow is included in jurisprudence as an example of fraud: "If . . . Bob promised to pour the man a glass of Pappy Van Winkle but gave him a slug of Old Crow instead, well, that would be fraud." United States v. Takhalov, 827 F.3d 1307, 1313, n.5, 6 (11th Cir. 2016) (Thapar, J., sitting by designation).

3. Beam-Suntory, Inc., "Old Crow Wins Another Decision" advertisement, *LIFE*, Sept. 15, 1952, 84.

4. W. A. Gaines & Co. v. Rock Spring Distilling Co., 226 F. 531, 534 (6th Cir. 1915).

5. W. A. Gaines & Co. v. E. Whyte Grocery, Fruit & Wine Co., 107 Mo. App. 507, 81 S.W. 648, 652 (1904).

6. *Whyte Grocery*, 81 S.W. at 652.

7. *Whyte Grocery*, 81 S.W. at 652.

8. *Whyte Grocery*, 81 S.W. at 652.

9. *Whyte Grocery*, 81 S.W. at 652–53.

10. W. A. Gaines & Co. v. Kahn, 155 F. 639, 640–41 (E.D. Mo. 1907).

11. Kahn v. W. A. Gaines & Co., 161 F. 495, 497–98 (8th Cir. 1908), *cert denied* 212 U.S. 572 (1908) and 241 U.S. 668 (1916).

12. *Kahn*, 161 F. at 497–98.

13. W. A. Gaines & Co. v. Rock Spring Distilling Co., 202 F. 989, 993 (W.D. Ky. 1913) (again claiming exclusive continuous use since 1835).

14. W. A. Gaines & Co. v. Leslie, 25 Misc. 20, 54 N.Y.S. 421, 422 (1898).

15. *Whyte Grocery*, 81 S.W. at 648.

16. *Whyte Grocery*, 81 S.W. at 655.

17. *Whyte Grocery*, 81 S.W. at 656.

18. *See* Gaines v. Knecht, 27 App. D.C. 530 (1906) ("Raven Valley Whisky"); and Gaines v. Carlton Importation Co., 27 App. D.C. 571 (1906) ("Old Jay").

19. *W. A. Gaines*, 155 F. at 642; *Kahn*, 161 F. at 501.

20. *W. A. Gaines*, 155 F. at 643.

21. *Kahn*, 161 F. at 499, Exhibit No. 6.

22. *W. A. Gaines*, 155 F. at 639.

23. *W. A. Gaines*, 155 F. at 642, 644.

24. *W. A. Gaines*, 155 F. at 644–45.

25. *W. A. Gaines*, 155 F. at 645.

26. W. A. *Gaines*, 155 F. at 645.

27. *Kahn*, 161 F. at 497–98.

28. *Kahn*, 161 F. at 498.

29. *Kahn*, 161 F. at 498.

30. *Kahn*, 161 F. at 500–501.

31. *Kahn*, 161 F. at 501.

32. Kentucky Distilleries & Warehouse Co. v. Wathen, 110 F. 641, 645 (C.C. W.D. Ky. 1901).

33. W. A. Gaines & Co. v. Rock Spring Distilling Co., 179 F. 544 (W.D. Ky. 1910).

34. W. A. Gaines & Co. v. Rock Spring Distilling Co., 202 F. 989, 990 (W.D. Ky. 1913).

35. *Rock Spring*, 202 F. at 992–93.

36. *Rock Spring*, 202 F. at 993.

37. *Rock Spring*, 202 F. at 993.

38. W. A. Gaines & Co. v. Rock Spring Distilling Co., 226 F. 531 (6th Cir. 1915).

39. *Rock Spring*, 226 F. at 542.

40. *Rock Spring*, 226 F. at 541.

41. *Rock Spring*, 226 F. at 539.

42. *Rock Spring*, 226 F. at 539.

43. *Rock Spring*, 226 F. at 542.

44. Rock Spring Distilling Co. v. W. A. Gaines & Co., 246 U.S. 312 (1918).

45. *Rock Spring*, 246 U.S. at 322.

46. S.J. Res. 17, 40 Stat. 1050 (1917).

47. 41 Stat. 305 (1919).

48. Rare Breed Distilling LLC v. Jim Beam Brands Co., No. 3:11-cv-00292-H, (W.D. Ky.) (Complaint filed May 13, 2011).

49. *Rare Breed*, No. 3:11-cv-00292-H, (W.D. Ky.), at Docket No. 1, Complaint ¶ 12.

50. *Rare Breed*, No. 3:11-cv-00292-H, (W.D. Ky.), at Docket No. 23, Transcript of July 18, 2011, hearing 11–12, 46.

51. *Rare Breed*, No. 3:11-cv-00292-H, (W.D. Ky.), at Docket No. 1, Complaint ¶¶ 13, 14, 15, 16.

52. *Rare Breed*, No. 3:11-cv-00292-H, (W.D. Ky.), at Docket No. 1, Complaint, Exhibit B (2006 promotion) and Exhibit D (2007 promotion).

53. *Rare Breed*, No. 3:11-cv-00292-H, (W.D. Ky.), at Docket No. 1, Complaint ¶ 17.

54. *Rare Breed*, No. 3:11-cv-00292-H, (W.D. Ky.), at Docket No. 1, Complaint, Exhibit G (2011 website home page).

55. Old Crow Reserve Press Release, Armstrong Associates, June 29, 2010.

56. *Rare Breed*, No. 3:11-cv-00292-H, Docket No. 1, Complaint ¶ 18, Exhibit F.

57. *Rare Breed*, No. 3:11-cv-00292-H, at Docket No. 1, Complaint.

58. *Rare Breed*, No. 3:11-cv-00292-H, at Docket No. 11, Answer and Verified Counterclaim, June 13, 2011.

59. *Rare Breed*, No. 3:11-cv-00292-H, at Docket No. 23, Transcript of July 18, 2011, Hearing, 3.

60. *Rare Breed*, No. 3:11-cv-00292-H, at Docket No. 22, July 22, 2011, Order.

61. *Rare Breed*, No. 3:11-cv-00292-H, at Docket No. 28, Rare Breed Distilling LLC's Preliminary Injunction Hearing Brief, 2, 9, and App. 4.

62. *Rare Breed*, No. 3:11-cv-00292-H, at Docket No. 32, Agreed Order of Dismissal with Prejudice, entered Aug. 10, 2011.

63. DISCUS Ruling, Aug. 2011, available at http://www.discus.org/assets/1/7/Wild_Turkey_Write-Up.pdf.

5. Bourbon Expands Trade Name Rights

1. Frazier v. Dowling, 18 Ky. L. Rptr. 1109, 39 S.W. 45 (1897).

2. *Frazier*, 39 S.W. at 45–46.

3. *Frazier*, 39 S.W. at 46.

4. *Frazier*, 39 S.W. at 46; John Dowling v. G. G. Frazier, Jefferson County Circuit Court, Chancery Div., Oct. 14, 1892, dep. of John Dowling at 5.

5. *Frazier*, 39 S.W. at 46; *Dowling v. Frazier* (Jefferson Circuit Court), dep. of John Dowling at 6–7. The purchase price was $17,074.

6. *Dowling v. Frazier* (Jefferson Circuit Court), dep. of John Dowling at 7.

7. *Frazier*, 39 S.W. at 46.

8. *Frazier*, 39 S.W. at 46; *Dowling v. Frazier* (Jefferson Circuit Court), dep. of John Dowling at 3.

9. *Frazier*, 39 S.W. at 46.

10. *Frazier*, 39 S.W. at 46; *Dowling v. Frazier* (Jefferson Circuit Court), Exhibit, Apr. 28, 1890, letter from William J. Waterfill.

11. *Frazier*, 39 S.W. at 46.

12. *Dowling v. Frazier* (Jefferson Circuit Court), dep. of John Dowling at 8–9.

13. *Frazier*, 39 S.W. at 46.

14. *Frazier*, 39 S.W. at 46.

15. *Frazier*, 39 S.W. at 46.

16. *Frazier*, 39 S.W. at 46.

17. *Dowling v. Frazier* (Jefferson Circuit Court), Exhibit D.

18. *Dowling v. Frazier* (Jefferson Circuit Court), Exhibit 21.

19. *Frazier*, 39 S.W. at 46.

20. *Frazier v. Dowling*, 39 S.W. at 46.

21. National Distillers Products Corp. v. K. Taylor Distilling Co., 31 F. Supp. 611 (E.D. Ky. 1940).

22. *National Distillers*, 31 F. Supp. at 612–13.

23. *National Distillers*, 31 F. Supp. at 613.

24. *National Distillers*, 31 F. Supp. at 613.

25. *National Distillers*, 31 F. Supp. at 613.

26. *National Distillers*, 31 F. Supp. at 613.

27. *National Distillers*, 31 F. Supp. at 613.

28. *National Distillers*, 31 F. Supp. at 613.

29. *National Distillers*, 31 F. Supp. at 613.

30. *National Distillers*, 31 F. Supp. at 612–13.

31. *National Distillers*, 31 F. Supp. at 614.

32. *National Distillers*, 31 F. Supp. at 614.

33. *National Distillers*, 31 F. Supp. at 614.

34. *National Distillers*, 31 F. Supp. at 614.

35. *National Distillers*, 31 F. Supp. at 614.

36. *National Distillers*, 31 F. Supp. at 614–15.

37. *National Distillers*, 31 F. Supp. at 613, 615.

38. *National Distillers*, 31 F. Supp. at 615–16.

39. *National Distillers*, 31 F. Supp. at 616.

40. Baumer v. Franklin County Distilling Co., 135 F.2d 384, 386 (6th Cir. 1943).

41. *Baumer*, 135 F.2d at 387.

42. Country Distillers Products, Inc. v. Samuels, Inc., 309 Ky. 262, 217 S.W.2d 216 (1948).

43. *Country Distillers*, 217 S.W.2d at 216–17.

44. *Country Distillers*, 217 S.W.2d at 217.

45. Country Distillers Products, Inc. v. Old Samuels Distillery, Inc., Nelson Circuit Court, Feb. 13, 1947, dep. of T. William Samuels at 17.

46. *Country Distillers*, 217 S.W.2d at 217.

47. *Country Distillers*, 217 S.W.2d at 217.

48. *Country Distillers v. Old Samuels* (Nelson Circuit Court), dep. of T. William Samuels at 18; Answer at 3.

49. *Country Distillers v. Old Samuels* (Nelson Circuit Court), dep. of T. William Samuels at 18.

50. *Country Distillers v. Old Samuels* (Nelson Circuit Court), dep. of T. William Samuels at 20, 26.

51. *Country Distillers v. Old Samuels* (Nelson Circuit Court), dep. of T. William Samuels at 27.

52. *Country Distillers*, 217 S.W.2d at 217–18.

53. *Country Distillers*, 217 S.W.2d at 220.

54. *Country Distillers*, 217 S.W.2d at 220–21.

55. John P. Dant Distillery Co. v. Schenley Distillers, Inc., 189 F. Supp. 821 (W.D. Ky. 1960).

56. *Dant*, 189 F. Supp. at 823–24.

57. *Dant*, 189 F. Supp. at 823.

58. *Dant*, 189 F. Supp. at 823–24.

59. *Dant*, 189 F. Supp. at 824.

60. *Dant*, 189 F. Supp. at 825.

61. *Dant*, 189 F. Supp. at 825–26.

62. *Dant*, 189 F. Supp. at 827.

63. "The Manufacture of Whisky in Kentucky," *Wine and Spirit Bulletin* 19, no. 6, June 1, 1905, 22–29.

64. "Manufacture of Whisky in Kentucky," *supra*, at 22.

65. "Manufacture of Whisky in Kentucky," *supra*, at 24.

66. "Manufacture of Whisky in Kentucky," *supra*, at 24.

67. "Manufacture of Whisky in Kentucky," *supra*, at 26.

68. "Manufacture of Whisky in Kentucky," *supra*, at 26.

69. "Manufacture of Whisky in Kentucky," *supra*, at 26.

70. "Manufacture of Whisky in Kentucky," *supra*, at 26.

71. Not to be confused with the Distillers' and Cattle Feeders' Trust—*the* Whiskey Trust—organized in 1887 by Joseph Greenhut in Peoria, Illinois, and modeled after John D. Rockefeller's Standard Oil Trust. Greenhut's Whiskey Trust was the first (temporarily) successful effort to monopolize whiskey production, but it tended to focus on large distilleries in Illinois and Indiana, and the producers of straight whiskey in Kentucky tended to evade its grasp. The Kentucky Distilleries and Warehouse Company was the more local effort to consolidate and monopolize whiskey production.

72. "Manufacture of Whisky in Kentucky," *supra*, at 26, 28.

73. "Manufacture of Whisky in Kentucky," *supra*, at 26, 28.

74. Wathen v. Kentucky Distilleries & Warehouse Co., 140 Ky. 417, 131 S.W. 202 (1910).

75. J. B. Wathen v. Kentucky Distilleries & Warehouse Co., No. 25068, Jefferson Circuit Court, Chancery Branch, Second Div., Sept. 7, 1909, Order and Oct. 3, 1909, Judgment.

76. *Wathen*, 131 S.W. at 203.

77. Kentucky Distilleries & Warehouse Co. v. Wathen, 110 F. 641 (C.C. W.D. Ky. 1901).

78. *Kentucky Distilleries* & Warehouse Co., 110 F. at 643.

79. *Kentucky Distilleries* & Warehouse Co., 110 F. at 643.

80. *Kentucky Distilleries* & Warehouse Co., 110 F. at 643–44.

81. *Kentucky Distilleries* & Warehouse Co., 110 F. at 643–44.

82. *Kentucky Distilleries* & Warehouse Co., 110 F. at 644.

83. *Kentucky Distilleries* & Warehouse Co., 110 F. at 645.

84. *Kentucky Distilleries* & Warehouse Co., 110 F. at 642–43.

85. *Kentucky Distilleries* & Warehouse Co., 110 F. at 642.

86. *Kentucky Distilleries* & Warehouse Co., 110 F. at 645.

87. Churchill Downs Distilling Co. v. Churchill Downs, Inc., 262 Ky. 567, 90 S.W.2d 1041 (1936).

88. *Churchill Downs Distilling*, 90 S.W.2d at 1042.

89. *Churchill Downs Distilling*, 90 S.W.2d at 1042.

90. *Churchill Downs Distilling*, 90 S.W.2d at 1042.

91. *Churchill Downs Distilling*, 90 S.W.2d at 1042.

92. *Churchill Downs Distilling*, 90 S.W.2d at 1043.

93. *Churchill Downs Distilling*, 90 S.W.2d at 1043.

94. *Churchill Downs Distilling*, 90 S.W.2d at 1042.

95. *Churchill Downs Distilling*, 90 S.W.2d at 1042–43.

96. *Churchill Downs Distilling*, 90 S.W.2d at 1044–45.

97. *Churchill Downs Distilling*, 90 S.W.2d at 1045.

6. Bourbon Marketers on Puffery, Exaggeration

1. Carlill v. Carbolic Smoke Ball Co. (1839) 1 Q.B. 256 (C.A.); Dimmock v. Hallett, (1866) L. R. 2 Ch. App. 21.

2. J. Thomas McCarthy, *McCarthy on Trademarks and Unfair Competition*, § 27:38 (5th ed., 2017).

3. Brown-Forman Corp. v. Barton Inc., No. 3:03-cv-00648-JBC (W.D. Ky.) (Complaint filed Oct. 23, 2003), Docket No. 38-2, Memorandum in Support of Motion for Summary Judgment, 4.

4. *Brown-Forman*, No. 3:03-cv-00648-JBC, Docket No. 38-2, Memorandum in Support of Motion for Summary Judgment, 4.

5. *Brown-Forman*, No. 3:03-cv-00648-JBC, Docket No. 38-2, Memorandum in Support of Motion for Summary Judgment, 4.

6. *Brown-Forman*, No. 3:03-cv-00648-JBC, at Docket No. 42, Defendants' Opposition to Plaintiff Brown-Forman's Motion for Summary Judgment on Barton's Counterclaim, 10.

7. *Brown-Forman*, No. 3:03-cv-00648-JBC, at Docket No. 121, May 11, 2004, Final Judgment, 1–2.

8. Ortved, "Making of Fine Kentucky Whisky," 20.

9. Salters v. Beam Suntory, Inc., Case No. 4:14cv659-RH/CAS, 2015 WL 2124939 (N.D. Fla. May 1, 2015).

10. *Salters*, 2015 WL 2124939 at *2 (quoting *Oxford English Dictionary*, 9th ed. [1971], 1251).

11. *Salters*, 2015 WL 2124939 at *2.

12. *Salters*, 2015 WL 2124939 at *2.

13. *Salters*, 2015 WL 2124939 at *2.

14. *Salters*, 2015 WL 2124939 at *2-3.

15. *Salters*, 2015 WL 2124939 at *3.

16. Nowrouzi v. Maker's Mark Distillery, Inc., Civil No. 14cv2885 JAH (NLS), 2015 WL 4523551 (S.D. Cal. July 27, 2015).

17. *Nowrouzi*, 2015 WL 4523551 at *1 (quoting and citing Complaint, ¶¶ 21, 34, 36).

18. *Nowrouzi*, 2015 WL 4523551 at *1 (quoting and citing Complaint, ¶¶ 35, 65).

19. *Nowrouzi*, 2015 WL 4523551 at *2.

20. *Nowrouzi*, 2015 WL 4523551 at *2 (citing 27 U.S.C. § 205; 27 C.F.R. § 13.1, 13.21, 5.65[a]).

21. *Nowrouzi*, 2015 WL 4523551 at *3-4.

22. *Nowrouzi*, 2015 WL 4523551 at *4-5.

23. *Nowrouzi*, 2015 WL 4523551 at *5.

24. *Nowrouzi*,) 2015 WL 4523551 at *5 (internal citations omitted).

25. *Nowrouzi*, 2015 WL 4523551 at *5.

26. *Nowrouzi*, 2015 WL 4523551 at *6.

27. *Nowrouzi*, 2015 WL 4523551 at *5.

28. *Nowrouzi*, 2015 WL 4523551 at *7.

29. Gaines & Co. v. Sroufe, 117 F. 965, 966 (C. C. N.D. Cal. 1901).

30. W. A. Gaines & Co. v. Turner-Looker Co., 204 F. 553, 555 (6th Cir. 1913) *appeal dismissed* 231 U.S. 769 (1914).

31. *Turner-Looker*, 204 F. at 555.

32. *Turner-Looker*, 204 F. at 556.

33. *Turner-Looker*, 204 F. at 556.

34. *Turner-Looker*, 204 F. at 557.

35. *Turner-Looker*, 204 F. at 558.

36. *Turner-Looker*, 204 F. at 559.

37. Krauss v. Jos. R. Peebles' Sons Co., 58 F. 585, 593–94 (S.D. Ohio 1893); Brown-Forman Corp. v. Barton Inc., No. 3:03-cv-00648-JBC (W.D. Ky.).

7. Bourbon Leads the Nation to Consumer Protection

1. Peacock Distillery Co. v. Commonwealth, 25 Ky. L. Rptr. 1778, 78 S.W. 893, 895 (1904).

2. City of Henderson v. Robinson, 152 Ky. 245, 153 S.W. 224 (1913); City of Henderson v. Kentucky Peerless Distilling Co., 161 Ky. 1, 170 S.W. 210 (1914); and Kraver v. Smith, 164 Ky. 674, 177 S.W. 286 (1915).

3. *Robinson*, 153 S.W. at 225.

4. Thomas' Adm'r v. Eminence Distilling Co., 151 Ky. 29, 151 S.W. 47 (1912); Kentucky Distilleries & Warehouse Co. v. Commonwealth, 24 Ky. L. Rptr. 2154, 73 S.W. 746 (1903); and Commonwealth v. Kentucky Distilleries & Warehouse Co., 154 Ky. 787, 159 S.W. 570 (1913).

5. Trumbo's Adm'x v. W. A. Gaines & Co., 33 Ky. L. Rptr. 415, 109 S.W. 1188, 1189 (1908).

6. *Trumbo's Adm'x*, 109 S.W. at 1189.

7. W. A. Gaines & Co. v. Johnson, 32 Ky. L. Rptr. 58, 133 Ky. 507, 105 S.W. 381 (1907).

8. *W. A. Gaines*, 105 S.W. at 383.

9. *W. A. Gaines*, 105 S.W. at 384.

10. Dryden v. H. E. Pogue Distillery Co., 26 Ky. L. Rptr. 528, 82 S.W. 262 (1904).

11. *Dryden*, 82 S.W. at 262.

12. *Dryden*, 82 S.W. at 262.

13. The boy's story is told in a trio of cases, Wells v. Kentucky Distilleries & Warehouse Co., 144 Ky. 438, 138 S.W. 278 (1911); Kentucky Distilleries & Warehouse Co. v. Wells, 149 Ky. 275, 148 S.W. 375 (1912); and Kentucky Distilleries & Warehouse Co. v. Wells, 149 Ky. 287, 148 S.W. 381 (1912), including a detailed description of the slop tubs and distillery's slop procedures.

14. Kentucky Distilleries & Warehouse Co. v. Schreiber, 24 Ky. L. Rptr. 2236, 73 S.W. 769, 769–70 (1903).

15. Schreiber, 73 S.W. at 770.

16. Kentucky Distilleries & Warehouse Co. v. Johnson, 193 Ky. 669, 237 S.W. 3 (1922).

17. *Johnson*, 237 S.W. at 4.

18. *Johnson*, 237 S.W. at 3.

19. *Johnson*, 237 S.W. at 3.

20. *Johnson*, 237 S.W. at 3.

21. *Johnson*, 237 S.W. at 3.

22. *Johnson*, 237 S.W. at 3.

23. *Johnson*, 237 S.W. at 5.

24. Anderson & Nelson Distilling Co. v. Hair, 19 Ky. L. Rptr. 1822, 103 Ky. 196, 44 S.W. 658 (1898); Belle of Nelson Distilling Co. v. Riggs, 20 Ky. L. Rptr. 499, 104 Ky. 1, 45 S.W. 99 (1898); Old Times Distillery Co. v. Zehnder, 21 Ky. L. Rptr. 753, 52 S.W. 1051 (1899); Kentucky Distilleries & Warehouse Co. v. Leonard, 25 Ky. L. Rptr. 2046, 79 S.W. 281 (1904); Carey v. W. B. Samuels & Co., 28 Ky. L. Rptr. 6, 139 Ky. 623, 88 S.W. 1052 (1905); Wood's Adm'x v. Daviess County Distilling Co., 31 Ky. L. Rptr. 511, 102 S.W. 813 (1907); Eagle Distillery v. Hardy, 120 S.W. 336 (Ky. 1909); Enos v. Kentucky Distilleries & Warehouse Co., 189 F. 342, 111 C.C.A. 74 (6th Cir. 1911).

25. Bottled-in-Bond Act of 1897, ch. 379, 29 Stat. 626.

26. Bottled-in-Bond Act of 1897, ch. 379, 29 Stat. 626.

27. 27 C.F.R. § 5.42(b)(3).

28. W. A. Gaines & Co. v. Turner-Looker Co., 204 F. 553, 557 (6th Cir. 1913) *appeal dismissed* 231 U.S. 769 (1914).

29. *Turner-Looker*, 204 F. at 557.

30. *Turner-Looker*, 204 F. at 558.

31. Wathen v. Kentucky Distilleries & Warehouse Co., 140 Ky. 417, 131 S.W. 202, 203 (1910).

32. *Wathen*, 131 S.W. at 204.

33. *Wathen* 131 S.W. at 203.

34. *Wathen* 131 S.W. at 203.

35. *Wathen* 131 S.W. at 203.

36. *Turner-Looker*, 204 F. at 557.

37. *Turner-Looker*, 204 F. at 557–58.

38. *See* E. H. Taylor, Jr. & Sons Co. v. Marion E. Taylor, 27 Ky. L. Rptr., 124 Ky. 173, 85 S.W. 1085, 1086 (1905).

39. *Peck v. Tribune Co.*, 154 F. 330, 331 (1907), *reversed* 214 U.S. 185 (1909).

40. Samuel Hopkins Adams, *The Great American Fraud: Articles on the Nostrum Evil and Quacks.*, 4th ed., reprinted from *Collier's Weekly* (Chicago: P. F. Collier's, 1905).

41. Adams, *The Great American Fraud, supra*, at 11.

42. Adams, *The Great American Fraud, supra*, at 18, 19.

43. Cullinan *ex rel.* New York v. Paxson, 100 N.Y. App. Div. 515, 91 N.Y.S. 1092 (1905).

44. *Cullinan*, 100 N.Y. App. Div. 515.

45. United States v. 50 Barrels of Whisky, 165 F. 966, 967 (D. Md. 1908).

46. *50 Barrels of Whisky*, 165 F. at 970.

47. E. H. Taylor, Jr. & Sons Co. v. Marion E. Taylor, 27 Ky. L. Rptr., 124 Ky. 173, 85 S.W. 1085, 1086 (1905).

48. *E. H. Taylor, Jr. & Sons Co. v. Marion E. Taylor*, No. 10782, Jefferson Circuit Court, Chancery Branch, 1st Div.

49. *E. H. Taylor, Jr. & Sons*, No. 10782, May 21, 1897, dep. of E. H. Taylor Jr., at 15.

50. *E. H. Taylor, Jr. & Sons*, No. 10782, Mar. 29, 1913 dep. of Dion L. Johnson, at 4–7, Exhibit 1.

51. *E. H. Taylor, Jr. & Sons*, 85 S.W. at 1085.

52. E. H. Taylor, Jr. & Sons, 85 S.W. at 1085. (in today's dollars, a multimillion dollar claim).

53. E. H. Taylor, Jr. & Sons, 85 S.W. at 1086.

54. E. H. Taylor, Jr. & Sons, 85 S.W. at 1088.

55. E. H. Taylor, Jr. & Sons, 85 S.W. at 1088.

56. E. H. Taylor, Jr. & Sons, 85 S.W. at 1086.

57. E. H. Taylor, Jr. & Sons, 85 S.W. at 1087.

58. E. H. Taylor, Jr. & Sons, 85 S.W. at 1087–88.

59. E. H. Taylor, Jr. & Sons, 85 S.W. at 1088.

60. E. H. Taylor, Jr. & Sons, 85 S.W. at 1088.

61. In re Wright, 33 App. D.C. 510 (1909).

62. *In re Wright*, 33 App. D.C. at 512.

63. *In re Wright*, 33 App. D.C. at 514.

64. *In re Wright*, 33 App. D.C. at 510 (quoting 26 Ops. Atty. Gen. 216).

65. *In re Wright*, 33 App. D.C. at 514.

66. *In re Wright*, 33 App. D.C. at 514–15.

67. *In re Wright*, 33 App. D.C. at 515–16. Indeed, other contemporary Taylor brands included G. W. Taylor, G. O. Taylor, Taylor (yet another Taylor but this one in New York), and Geo. W. Taylor. *See* E. H. Taylor Jr. v. Marion E. Taylor, No. 10782, Jefferson Circuit Court, Apr. 14, 1898, dep. of J. Swigert Taylor, at 186.

68. *In re Wright*, 33 App. D.C. at 516.

69. Maker's Mark Distillery, Inc. v. Diageo North Am., Inc., 679 F.3d 410, 416 (6th Cir. 2012) citing Willis, "What Whiskey Is," *McClure's Magazine* 34 (1910): 687, 699 (1910).

70. *Maker's Mark*, 679 F.3d at 416.

71. *Maker's Mark*, 679 F.3d at 416.

72. *Maker's Mark*, 679 F.3d at 416.

73. *Maker's Mark*, 679 F.3d at 416.

8. Behind-the-Scenes Story of Prohibition

1. *See, e.g.,* Fred Minnick, *Whiskey Women: The Untold Story of How Women Saved Bourbon, Scotch, and Irish Whiskey* (Dulles va: Potomac Books, 2013); Michael Veach, *Kentucky Bourbon Whiskey: An American Heritage* (Lexington: University Press of Kentucky, 2013); and Colin Spoelman and David Haskell, *Dead Distillers: A History of the Upstarts and Outlaws Who Made American Spirits* (New York: Abrams, 2016), respectively.

2. Wathen, Mueller & Co. v. Commonwealth, 133 Ky. 94, 116 S.W. 336, 337 (1909).

3. *See Wathen, Mueller & Co.*, 116 S.W. at 338.

4. *See Wathen, Mueller* & Co., 116 S.W. at 338–39.

5. *See Wathen, Mueller* & Co., 116 S.W. at 339.

6. *See Wathen, Mueller* & Co., 116 S.W. at 337.

7. *See Wathen, Mueller* & Co., 116 S.W. at 338.

8. *See Wathen, Mueller* & Co., 116 S.W. at 338.

9. *See Wathen, Mueller* & Co., 116 S.W. at 337.

10. *See Wathen, Mueller* & Co., 116 S.W. at 338.

11. Rush v. Denhardt, 138 Ky. 238, 127 S.W. 785 (1910).

12. *Rush*, 127 S.W. at 786.

13. *Rush*, 127 S.W. at 785.

14. *Rush*, 127 S.W. at 786.

15. Wathen v. Commonwealth, 171 Ky. 194, 188 S.W. 346 (1916).

16. *Wathen*, 188 S.W. at 346.

17. *Wathen*, 188 S.W. at 346–47.

18. *Wathen*, 188 S.W. at 347.

19. *Wathen*, 188 S.W. at 347.

20. *Wathen*, 188 S.W. at 347.

21. *Wathen*, 188 S.W. at 347–48.

22. Food and Fuel Control (Lever) Act of 1917, ch. 52, 40 Stat. 276; War-Time Prohibition Act, ch. 212, 40 Stat. 1045 (1918).

23. S.J. Res. 17, 40 Stat. 1050 (1917); U.S. Const. amend. 18.

24. Volstead Act, ch. 85, 41 Stat. 305 (1919).

25. W. A. Gaines & Co. v. Holmes, 154 Ga. 344, 114 S.E. 327 (1922).

26. *W. A. Gaines & Co.*, 114 S.E. at 327.

27. *W. A. Gaines & Co.*, 114 S.E. at 327–28.

28. *W. A. Gaines & Co.*, 114 S.E. at 329 (quoting Volstead Act, § 3).

29. *W. A. Gaines & Co.*, 114 S.E. at 328 (quoting Ga. Laws Extraordinary Session 1917, § 20, p. 16).

30. *W. A. Gaines & Co.*, 114 S.E. at 332 (1922).

31. Wathen v. Commonwealth, 211 Ky. 586, 277 S.W. 839 (1925).

32. *Wathen*, 277 S.W. at 840.

33. *Wathen*, 277 S.W. at 840.

34. U.S. Const. amend. 21 (except in the District of Columbia, which needed to repeal the Sheppard Act and did so on Mar. 1, 1934, eighty-five days after Prohibition had been repealed in the rest of the nation, giving the Annapolis bourbon destination bar and restaurant Dry 85 a great story).

35. Age Int'l, Inc. v. Miller, 830 F. Supp. 1484 (N.D. Ga. 1993).

36. *Age Int'l*, 830 F. Supp. at 1487.

37. *Age Int'l*, 830 F. Supp. at 1487.

38. Ripy Bros. Distillers, Inc. v. Commissioner of Internal Revenue, 11 T.C. 326, 330 (1948).

39. Emergency Price Control Act of 1942, ch. 26, 56 Stat. 23.

40. *See* Dowling Bros. Distilling Co. v. United States, 153 F.2d 1946 (6th Cir. 1946).

41. Alcoholic Beverage Control Board v. Pebbleford Distillers, Inc., 302 Ky. 96, 193 S.W.2d 1019 (1946).

42. Maxwell's Pic-Pac, Inc. v. Dehner, 739 F.3d 936 (6th Cir. 2014).

43. *Maxwell's Pic-Pac*, 739 F.3d at 938.

44. Bd. of Trs. of Town of New Castle v. Scott, 101 S.W. 944 (Ky. 1907).

45. *Maxwell's Pic-Pac*, 739 F.3d at 938–39.

46. Maxwell's Pic-Pac, Inc. v. Dehner, 887 F. Supp. 2d 733, 739 (W.D. Ky. 2012) (quoting Ky. Liquor Control Comm., *Report of the Liquor Control. Comm.*, 3–4 [1933]).

47. *Maxwell's Pic-Pac*, 739 F.3d at 939 (quoting 1938 Ky. Acts c. 2 art. II § 54[8]) (codified as Ky. Stat. § 2554–154[8] [1939]).

48. *Maxwell's Pic-Pac*, 739 F.3d at 940.

49. *Maxwell's Pic-Pac*, 739 F.3d at 940–41.

50. *Maxwell's Pic-Pac*, 739 F.3d at 940.

51. Commonwealth of Ky. ABC Bd. v. Burke, 481 S.W.2d 52 (Ky. 1972).

52. Kentucky House Bill 100, which was signed by Kentucky governor Matt Bevin in June 2017 at the Heaven Hill Bourbon Heritage Center in Bardstown, permits private sales of "vintage distilled spirits" to specially licensed retailers. *See* Ky. Rev. Stat. Ann. § 241.010(66) and § 243.232. Kentucky's Vintage Spirits Law went into effect on January 1, 2018, and should bolster Kentucky's status as a tourist destination for whiskey enthusiasts.

53. Ky. Rev. Stat. Ann. § 243.020(1).

54. Ky. Rev. Stat. Ann. § 243.990.

55. Ky. Rev. Stat. Ann. § 241.010(49).

56. 27 U.S.C. § 203.

57. *See, e.g.,* Bottle-Spot.com, Terms of Use, https://www.bottle-spot.com/terms-of-use.html, last accessed Mar. 19, 2018.

9. Law Reins in Fake Distillers, Secret Sourcing

1. H. E. Pogue Distillery Co. v. Paxton Bros. Co., 209 F. 108 (E.D. Ky. 1913).

2. *Pogue Distillery*, 209 F. at 109.

3. *Pogue Distillery*, 209 F. at 109.

4. *Pogue Distillery*, 209 F. at 109.

5. *Pogue Distillery*, 209 F. at 110.

6. *Pogue Distillery*, 209 F. at 110.

7. *Pogue Distillery*, 209 F. at 110.

8. *Pogue Distillery*, 209 F. at 110.

9. *Pogue Distillery*, 209 F. at 110.

10. See ch. 7.

11. Krauss v. Jos. R. Peebles' Sons Co., 58 F. 585 (S.D. Ohio 1893).

12. See ch. 3.

13. *Krauss*, 58 F. at 586.

14. *Krauss*, 58 F. at 590–91.

15. *Krauss*, 58 F. at 591.

16. *Krauss*, 58 F. at 592.

17. *Krauss*, 58 F. at 592.

18. *Krauss*, 58 F. at 593–94.

19. *Krauss*, 58 F. at 594.

20. *Krauss*, 58 F. at 594.

21. *Krauss*, 58 F. at 593–94.

22. *Krauss*, 58 F. at 594.

23. Maker's Mark Distillery, Inc. v. Diageo North Am., Inc., 679 F.3d 410, 416 (6th Cir. 2012) citing Willis, "What Whiskey Is," *McClure's Magazine* 34 (1910): 687, 699 (1910).

24. *See* Ripy Bros. Distillers, Inc. v. Commissioner of Internal Revenue, 11 T.C. 326 (1948).

25. *Ripy Bros.*, 11 T.C. at 327.

26. *Ripy Bros.*, 11 T.C. at 327.

27. *Ripy Bros.*, 11 T.C. at 329.

28. *Ripy Bros.*, 11 T.C. at 330, 332.

29. Gould v. Hiram Walker & Sons, Inc., 142 F.2d 544 (7th Cir. 1944).

30. *Gould*, 142 F.2d at 545.

31. *Gould*, 142 F.2d at 546.

32. *Gould*, 142 F.2d at 546.

33. *Gould*, 142 F.2d at 547.

34. Gould v. Hiram Walker & Sons, Inc., 266 F.2d 249 (7th Cir. 1959) ("Gould II").

35. *Gould II*, 266 F.2d at 251.

36. *Gould II*, 266 F.2d at 251.

37. *Gould II*, 266 F.2d at 251.

38. *Gould II*, 266 F.2d at 251.

39. Gould v. City Bank & Trust Co., 213 F.2d 314, 315 (4th Cir. 1954).

40. *Gould*, 213 F.2d at 317.

41. *See* McNair v. Templeton Rye Spirits, LLC, 2014-CH-14583 (Cir. Ct. Cook County, Ill.); Aliano v. Templeton Rye Spirits, LLC, 2014-CH-15667 (Cir. Ct. Cook County, Ill.); and Townsend v. Templeton Rye Spirits, LLC, CV 048581 (Iowa Dist. Ct., Polk County), removed and consolidated in the United States District Court for the Northern District of Illinois, No. 14-cv-07440.

10. Bourbon Drives Truth in Labeling

1. Mellwood Distilling Co. v. Harper, 167 F. 389, 392 (W.D. Ark. 1908).

2. *Mellwood*, 167 F. at 392.

3. *Mellwood*, 167 F. at 392.

4. *Mellwood*, 167 F. at 392.

5. *Mellwood*, 167 F. at 393.

6. *Mellwood*, 167 F. at 393–94.

7. *Mellwood*, 167 F. at 395.

8. Jack Daniel Distillery, Inc. v. Hoffman Distilling Co., 190 F. Supp. 841, 843 (W.D. Ky. 1960).

9. *Jack Daniel*, 190 F. Supp. at 843.

10. *Jack Daniel*, 190 F. Supp. at 844.

11. *Jack Daniel*, 190 F. Supp. at 843–44.

12. *Jack Daniel*, 190 F. Supp. at 843–44.

13. *Jack Daniel*, 190 F. Supp. at 845–46; *affirmed*, Jack Daniel Distiller, Lem Motlow, Prop., Inc. v. Hoffman Distilling Co., 298 F.2d 606 (6th Cir. 1962).

14. Brown-Forman Corp. v. Barton Inc., No. 3:03-cv-00648-JBC (W.D. Ky.).

15. *Brown-Forman*, No. 3:03-cv-00648-JBC at Docket No. 34, Answer to Amended Complaint and Counterclaim, ¶¶ 55–109.

16. *Brown-Forman*, No. 3:03-cv-00648-JBC at ¶¶ 89–95.

17. *Brown-Forman*, No. 3:03-cv-00648-JBC at ¶¶ 91.

18. *Brown-Forman*, No. 3:03-cv-00648-JBC at ¶¶ 95.

19. *Brown-Forman*, No. 3:03-cv-00648-JBC at Docket No. 34-6 (Exhibit 5 at 10).

20. *Brown-Forman*, No. 3:03-cv-00648-JBC at Docket No. 34-6 (Exhibit 5 at 10).

21. Krauss v. Jos. R. Peebles' Sons Co., 58 F. 585, 593–94 (S.D. Ohio 1893) (see ch. 9).

22. W. A. Gaines & Co. v. Turner-Looker Co., 204 F. 553 (6th Cir. 1913) (see ch. 6).

23. 27 U.S.C. § 205(e); Taylor Wine v. Dep't of Treasury, 509 F. Supp. 792, 794 (D.D.C. 1981).

24. 27 U.S.C. § 205(e).

25. 6 U.S.C. § 531(d); Treas. Order 120-01 (Dec. 10, 2013).

26. 27 U.S.C. § 205(e); 27 C.F.R. § 5.31(a).

27. *The Beverage Alcohol Manual (BAM): A Practical Guide, Basic Mandatory Labeling Information for DISTILLED SPIRITS*, vol. 2 (Washington DC: Department of the Treasury, 2012) ch. 1 § 1.

28. Ky. Rev. Stat. Ann. § 244.370.

29. *BAM*, ch. 1 §§ 2, 3, 15.

30. *BAM*, ch. 1 § 4.

31. *BAM*, ch. 1 § 4.

32. *BAM*, ch. 1 § 14.

33. *See* 27 C.F.R. § 5.23(a)(2).

34. *See BAM*, ch. 8.

35. *See BAM*, ch. 8.

36. *See also* 27 C.F.R. § 5.40(a)(1), (e)(1), (e)(2).

37. *See also* 27 C.F.R. § 5.40(a)(1), (e)(1), (e)(2).

38. 27 C.F.R. § 5.42(a)(1)-(7).

39. 27 C.F.R. § 5.42(b)(7).

40. 27 C.F.R. § 5.42(b)(4)-(5).

41. 27 C.F.R. § 5.42(b)(6).

TABLE OF AUTHORITIES

Cases

Age Int'l, Inc. v. Miller, 830 F. Supp. 1484 (N.D. Ga. 1993)

Alcoholic Beverage Control Board v. Pebbleford Distillers, Inc., 302 Ky. 96, 193 S.W.2d 1019 (1946)

Aliano v. Templeton Rye Spirits, LLC, 2014-CH-15667 (Cir. Ct. Cook County, Ill.)

Anderson & Nelson Distilling Co. v. Hair, 19 Ky. L. Rptr. 1822, 103 Ky. 196, 44 S.W. 658 (1898)

Baumer v. Franklin County Distilling Co., 135 F.2d 384 (6th Cir. 1943)

Bd. of Trs. of Town of New Castle v. Scott, 101 S.W. 944 (Ky. 1907)

Belle of Nelson Distilling Co. v. Riggs, 20 Ky. L. Rptr. 499, 104 Ky. 1, 45 S.W. 99 (1898)

Brown-Forman Corp. v. Barton Inc., No. 3:03-cv-00648-JBC (W.D. Ky.) (Complaint filed Oct. 23, 2003)

Brown-Forman Corp. v. Merrick, No. 2014-SC-000717-DG, 2017 WL 4296968 (Ky. Sept. 28, 2017)

Carey v. W. B. Samuels & Co., 28 Ky. L. Rptr. 6, 139 Ky. 623, 88 S.W. 1052 (1905)

Carlill v. Carbolic Smoke Ball Co. (1839) 1 Q.B. 256 (C.A.)

Churchill Downs Distilling Co. v. Churchill Downs, Inc., 262 Ky. 567, 90 S.W.2d 1041 (1936)

City of Henderson v. Kentucky Peerless Distilling Co., 161 Ky. 1, 170 S.W. 210 (1914)

City of Henderson v. Robinson, 152 Ky. 245, 153 S.W. 224 (1913)

Commonwealth of Ky. ABC Bd. v. Burke, 481 S.W.2d 52 (Ky. 1972)

Commonwealth v. Kentucky Distilleries & Warehouse Co., 154 Ky. 787, 159 S.W. 570 (1913)

Country Distillers Products, Inc. v. Old Samuels Distillery, Inc., Nelson Circuit Court

Country Distillers Products, Inc. v. Samuels, Inc., 309 Ky. 262, 217 S.W.2d 216 (1948)

Cullinan ex rel. New York v. Paxson, 100 N.Y. App. Div. 515, 91 N.Y.S. 1092 (1905)

Dep't of Revenue v. James B. Beam Distilling Co., 377 U.S. 341 (1964)

Dimmock v. Hallett (1866) L. R. 2 Ch. App. 21

Dowling Bros. Distilling Co. v. United States, 153 F.2d 1946 (6th Cir. 1946)

Dryden v. H. E. Pogue Distillery Co., 26 Ky. L. Rptr. 528, 82 S.W. 262 (1904)

E. & J. Gallo Winery v. Gallo Cattle Co., 1989 WL 159628 (E.D. Cal. 1989) *aff'd* 955 F.2d 1327 (9th Cir. 1992), opinion amended and superseded, 967 F.2d 1280 (9th Cir. 1992)

E. H. Taylor, Jr. v. Marion E. Taylor, No. 10782, Jefferson Circuit Court

E. H. Taylor, Jr. & Sons Co. v. Marion E. Taylor, 27 Ky. L. Rptr., 124 Ky. 173, 85 S.W. 1085 (1905)

Eagle Distillery v. Hardy, 120 S.W. 336 (Ky. 1909)

Eggnatz v. Kashi Co., No. 12-21678-CIV-LENARD/GOODMAN (S.D. Fla. 2016)

Ellison Educ. Equip., Inc. v. Tekservices, Inc., 903 F. Supp. 1350 (D. Neb. 1995)

Enos v. Kentucky Distilleries & Warehouse Co., 189 F. 342, C.C.A. 74 (6th Cir. 1911)

Federal Trade Commission v. Skechers U.S.A., Inc., No. 1:12-cv-01214 (N.D. Ohio 2012)

Frazier v. Dowling, 18 Ky. L. Rptr. 1109, 39 S.W. 45 (1897)

Gaines & Co. v. Sroufe, 117 F. 965 (C.C. N.D. Cal. 1901)

Gaines v. Carlton Importation Co., 27 App. D.C. 571 (1906)

Gaines v. Knecht, 27 App. D.C. 530 (1906)

Gemelas v. Dannon Co., Inc., No. 1:08-cv-00236 (N.D. Ohio 2010)

Geo. T. Stagg Co. v. E. H. Taylor & Sons, 24 Ky. L. Rptr. 495, 113 Ky. 709, 68 S.W. 862 (1902)

Geo. T. Stagg Co. v. Taylor, 16 Ky. L. Rptr. 213, 95 Ky. 651, 27 S.W. 247 (1894)

Gillette Co. v. Wilkinson Sword, Inc., No. 89 Civ. 3586, 1989 WL 82453 (S.D.N.Y. July 6, 1989)

Gould v. City Bank & Trust Co., 213 F.2d 314 (4th Cir. 1954)

Gould v. Hiram Walker & Sons, Inc., 142 F.2d 544 (7th Cir. 1944)

Gould v. Hiram Walker & Sons, Inc., 266 F.2d 249 (7th Cir. 1959)

H. E. Pogue Distillery Co. v. Paxton Bros. Co., 209 F. 108 (E.D. Ky. 1913)

In-N-Out Burgers v. Chadders Restaurant, No. 2:07-cv-394-TS, 2007 WL 1983813 (D. Utah June 29, 2007)

Interactive Prods. Corp. v. A2Z Mobile Office Solutions, Inc., 326 F.3d 687 (6th Cir. 2003)

J. B. Wathen v. Kentucky Distilleries & Warehouse Co., No. 25068, Jefferson Circuit Court, Chancery Branch, Second Div.

Jack Daniel Distillery, Inc. v. Hoffman Distilling Co., 190 F. Supp. 841 (W.D. Ky. 1960)

John Dowling v. G. G. Frazier, Jefferson County Circuit Court, Chancery Div.

John P. Dant Distillery Co. v. Schenley Distillers, Inc., 189 F. Supp. 821 (W.D. Ky. 1960)

Kahn v. W. A. Gaines & Co., 161 F. 495 (8th Cir. 1908), *cert denied* 212 U.S. 572 (1908)

Kentucky Distilleries & Warehouse Co. v. Commonwealth, 24 Ky. L. Rptr. 2154, 73 S.W. 746 (1903)

Kentucky Distilleries & Warehouse Co. v. Johnson, 193 Ky. 669, 237 S.W. 3 (1922)

Kentucky Distilleries & Warehouse Co. v. Leonard, 25 Ky. L. Rptr. 2046, 79 S.W. 281 (1904)

Kentucky Distilleries & Warehouse Co. v. Schreiber, 24 Ky. L. Rptr. 2236, 73 S.W. 769 (1903)

Kentucky Distilleries & Warehouse Co. v. Wathen, 110 F. 641 (C.C. W.D. Ky. 1901)

Kentucky Distilleries & Warehouse Co. v. Wells, 149 Ky. 275, 148 S.W. 375 (1912)

Kentucky Distilleries & Warehouse Co. v. Wells, 149 Ky. 287, 148 S.W. 381 (1912)

Koller v. Deoleo USA, Inc., No. 3:14-cv-02400 (N.D. Cal. 2014)

Krauss v. Jos. R. Peebles' Sons Co., 58 F. 585 (S.D. Ohio 1893)

Kraver v. Smith, 164 Ky. 674, 177 S.W. 286 (1915)

Kumar v. Safeway Inc., No. RG1472670 (Cal. Superior Ct., Alameda County 2014)

Kumar v. Salov North Am. Corp., No. 4:14-cv-02411-YGR (N.D. Cal., Jan. 27, 2017)

Levy v. Uri, 31 App. D.C. 441 (D.C. Cir. 1908)

In re Majestic Distilling Co., 420 F.2d 1086 (C.C.P.A. 1970)

Maker's Mark Distillery, Inc. v. Diageo North Am., Inc., 679 F.3d 410 (6th Cir. 2012)

Maker's Mark Distillery, Inc. v. Diageo North Am., Inc., 703 F. Supp. 2d 671 (W.D. Ky. 2010)

Mapp v. Ohio, 367 U.S. 643 (1961)

Maxwell's Pic-Pac, Inc. v. Dehner, 739 F.3d 936 (6th Cir. 2014)

Maxwell's Pic-Pac, Inc. v. Dehner, 887 F. Supp. 2d 733 (W.D. Ky. 2012)

McNair v. Templeton Rye Spirits, LLC, 2014-CH-14583 (Cir. Ct. Cook County, Ill.)

McNeil-PPC, Inc. v. Pfizer Inc., 351 F. Supp. 2d 226 (S.D.N.Y. 2005)

Mellwood Distilling Co. v. Harper, 167 F. 389 (W.D. Ark. 1908)

Merisant Co. v. McNeil Nutritionals, LLC, No. 04–5504 (E.D. Pa. 2007)

Mister Softee, Inc. v. Tsirkos, No. 14 Civ.1975(LTS)(RLE), 2014 WL 2535114 (S.D.N.Y. June 5, 2014)

Moseley v. V Secret Catalogue, Inc., 537 U.S. 418 (2003)

National Distillers Products Corp. v. K. Taylor Distilling Co., 31 F. Supp. 611 (E.D. Ky. 1940)

Newcomb-Buchanan Co. v. Baskett, 14 Bush 658, 77 Ky. 658 (1879)

Newcomb-Buchanan Co. v. Baskett, 4 Ky. L. Rptr. 828 (1883)

Newcomb-Buchanan Co. v. Baskett, Oldham Circuit Court, Civil Order Book, May 12, 1879

Nowrouzi v. Maker's Mark Distillery, Inc., Civil No. 14cv2885, 2015 WL 4523551 (S.D. Cal. July 27, 2015)

Old Times Distillery Co. v. Zehnder, 21 Ky. L. Rptr. 753, 52 S.W. 1051 (1899)

Peacock Distillery Co. v. Commonwealth, 25 Ky. L. Rptr. 1778, 78 S.W. 893 (1904)

Peck v. Tribune Co., 154 F. 330 (1907) *reversed* 214 U.S. 185 (1909)

Pepper v. Labrot, 8 F. 29 (C.C.D. Ky. 1881)

Pizza Hut, Inc. v. Papa John's Int'l, Inc., 227 F.3d 489 (5th Cir. 2000)

Rare Breed Distilling LLC v. Jim Beam Brands Co., No. 3:11-cv-00292-H (W.D. Ky.)

Rare Breed Distilling v. Heaven Hill Distilleries, No. C-09–04728 EDL, 2010 WL 335658 (N.D. Cal. Jan. 22, 2010)

Ripy Bros. Distillers, Inc. v. Commissioner of Internal Revenue, 11 T.C. 326 (1948)

Rock Spring Distilling Co. v. W. A. Gaines & Co., 246 U.S. 312 (1918)

Rush v. Denhardt, 138 Ky. 238, 127 S.W. 785 (1910)

Salters v. Beam Suntory, Inc., Case No. 4:14cv659-RH/CAS, 2015 WL 2124939 (N.D. Fla. May 1, 2015)

Sugar Assoc. v. McNeil Nutritionals, No. CV 04–1077DSF (C.D. Cal. 2008) Dismissal Order

Taylor v. Geo. T. Stagg Co., 18 Ky. L. Rptr. 680, 37 S.W. 954 (1896)

Taylor Wine v. Dep't of Treasury, 509 F. Supp. 792 (D.D.C. 1981)

Thomas' Adm'r v. Eminence Distilling Co., 151 Ky. 29, 151 S.W. 47 (1912)

Townsend v. Templeton Rye Spirits, LLC, CV 048581 (Iowa Dist. Ct., Polk County)

Trumbo's Adm'x v. W. A. Gaines & Co., 33 Ky. L. Rptr. 415, 109 S.W. 1188 (1908)

Under Armour, Inc. v. Nike, Inc., No. 1:13-cv-00571-ELH, 2014 WL 3810239 (D. Md. Feb. 10, 2014)

United States v. 50 Barrels of Whisky, 165 F. 966 (D. Md. 1908)

United States v. Takhalov, 827 F.3d 1307 (11th Cir. 2016)

V Secret Catalogue, Inc. v. Moseley, 259 F.3d 464 (6th Cir. 2001)

V Secret Catalogue, Inc. v. Moseley, 558 F. Supp. 2d 734 (W.D. Ky. 2008)

V Secret Catalogue, Inc. v. Moseley, 605 F.3d 382 (6th Cir. 2010)

V Secret Catalogue, Inc. v. Moseley, No. 3:98CV-395-S, 2000 WL 370525 (W.D. Ky. Feb. 9, 2000)

W. A. Gaines & Co. v. E. Whyte Grocery, Fruit & Wine Co., 107 Mo. App. 507, S.W. 648 (1904)

W. A. Gaines & Co. v. Holmes, 154 Ga. 344, 114 S.E. 327 (1922)

W. A. Gaines & Co. v. Johnson, 32 Ky. L. Rptr. 58, 133 Ky. 507, 105 S.W. 381 (1907)

W. A. Gaines & Co. v. Kahn, 155 F. 639 (E.D. Mo. 1907)

W. A. Gaines & Co. v. Leslie, 25 Misc. 20, 54 N.Y.S. 421 (1898)

W. A. Gaines & Co. v. Rock Spring Distilling Co., 179 F. 544 (W.D. Ky. 1910)

W. A. Gaines & Co. v. Rock Spring Distilling Co., 202 F. 989 (W.D. Ky. 1913)

W. A. Gaines & Co. v. Rock Spring Distilling Co., 226 F. 531 (6th Cir. 1915)

W. A. Gaines & Co. v. Turner-Looker Co., 204 F. 553 (6th Cir. 1913) *appeal dismissed* 231 U.S. 769 (1914)

Wathen v. Commonwealth, 171 Ky. 194, 188 S.W. 346 (1916)

Wathen v. Commonwealth, 211 Ky. 586, 277 S.W. 839 (1925)

Wathen v. Kentucky Distilleries & Warehouse Co., 140 Ky. 417, 131 S.W. 202 (1910)

Wathen, Mueller & Co. v. Commonwealth, 133 Ky. 94, 116 S.W. 336 (1909)

Wells v. Kentucky Distilleries & Warehouse Co., 144 Ky. 438, 138 S.W. 278 (1911)

Wood's Adm'x v. Daviess County Distilling Co., 31 Ky. L. Rptr. 511, 102 S.W. 813 (1907)

In re Wright, 33 App. D.C. 510 (1909)

Statutes, Regulations, and Resolutions

27 C.F.R. § 5.11

27 C.F.R. § 5.22

27 C.F.R. § 5.23

27 C.F.R. § 5.40

27 C.F.R. § 5.42

27 C.F.R. § 5.31(a)

6 U.S.C. § 531(d)

27 U.S.C. § 203

27 U.S.C. § 205

Bottled-in-Bond Act of 1897, ch. 379, 29 Stat. 626

Ch. 3915, 34 Stat. 768 (1906)

The Emergency Price Control Act of 1942, ch. 26, 56 Stat. 23

The Food and Fuel Control (Lever) Act of 1917, ch. 52, 40 Stat. 276

Ky. Rev. Stat. Ann. § 241.010(49), (66)

Ky. Rev. Stat. Ann. § 243.020(1)

Ky. Rev. Stat. Ann. § 243.232

Ky. Rev. Stat. Ann. § 243.990

Ky. Rev. Stat. Ann. § 244.370

Ky. Stat. § 2554–154(8) (1939)

S. Con. Res. 19, 88th Cong., 78 Stat. 1208 (May 4, 1964)

S.J. Res. 17, 40 Stat. 1050 (1917)

The Volstead Act, ch. 85, 41 Stat. 305 (1919)

J. M. Waterfill & Co. Distillers, 60
John P. Dant Distillery, 68–69
Johnson, Van, 46
Jose Curevo Reserva de La Familia, 37–40
Jos. R. Peebles' Sons Company, 126–28
J. S. Taylor Distillery, 32, 157n56
judges, biased, 107, 108–9
J. W. Dant Distillery. *See* Dant Distillery Co. Inc.

Kentucky: bourbon historically from, 10–11, 154n8; conditions favorable to bourbon production, 2, 3; migration of distillers to, 2, 3; use in name of bourbon, 16; vintage spirits law, 118, 122, 168n52
Kentucky Alcoholic Beverage Control Board (ABC), 114
Kentucky Bourbon Distillers, Ltd. *See* Willett Distillery
Kentucky Distilleries & Warehouse Co. *See* Kentucky Whiskey Trust
Kentucky Peerless Distilling Company, 86
Kentucky Whiskey Trust, 70–73, 88–90, 129, 136; compared to the Distillers' and Cattle Feeders' Trust, 162n71
Kirin Company, Ltd., 10
Krauss, Otto, 126–28
Kraver, Henry, 86
K. Taylor Distilling Co., 65–66
Ky. Credential, 72–73
Ky. Criterion, 71

labeling restrictions. *See* truth in labeling
Labrot & Graham, 6, 24–27, 126, 141–42
Lanham Act, 139
Lever Act. *See* Food and Fuel Control (Lever) Act of 1917
Limestone Branch Distillery, 59, 69
Liquor Outlet, 114–16
Listerine, 98
local option, 107–10, 114
Luxco, Inc., 10, 69, 123; tasting notes, Yellowstone bourbon, 69. *See also* Limestone Branch Distillery
Lux Row Distillery, 123–24

Maker's Mark Distillery: Country Distillers litigation, 66–68; handmade litigation, 20, 76–79; origins, 66–67; red wax litigation, 6, 36–41; tasting notes, 41, 42

The Manufacture of Liquors, Wines & Cordials without the Aid of Distillation, 4
marketing, 16–17, 19, 20; BAM, 143–46; brand name origin, 23, 24, 73; celebrity endorsement, 5; DISCUS, 19, 54, 57–58; Ezra Brooks, 137–39; "Give 'em the Bird," 54–58; imitation, 136–39; Jack Daniel's, 137–39; James Pepper, 26–27; Maker's Mark, 40, 158n93; Old Crow, 54–58; puffery, 75–83; vulgarity prohibited, 57–58; Wild Turkey, 54–58
Master Softee, 138
Maxwell's Pic-Pac, 114–16
Meadowlawn Distillery, 68
medicinal claims, 94–97, 147
medicinal licensing, 5, 111
medicinal use, 111–12
Mellwood Distillery, 135–36
merchant bottler. *See* sourced whiskey
MGP Ingredients, Inc., 132–33
Mill Wood Distilling Co., 136
Millwood, 135–36
Mister Softee, 138
Mitchell, W. F., 25, 27, 43, 46
Morris, Chris, 140
Moseley, Victor, 72

Nation, Carrie, 107, 166n1
National Distillers Products Corporation, 66
Nelson Distilling Co., 88
Newcomb-Buchanan Co., 29–31
Nike, 52
Noah's Mill Distilling Company, 134
Noe, Fred, 59
non-distiller producer. *See* sourced whiskey

O.F.C., 28–36; brand, 32, 35–36; distillery, 28–29; purchase by Duffy, 97, 157n75; purchase by Stagg, 31–32; purchase by Taylor, 28; *Taylor v. Stagg* litigation, 33–36
Office of Price Administration (OPA), 114, 130
old, as a description, 146
Old Charter Distillery, 99, 102
Old Crow bourbon: as example of fraud, 158n2; fame, 5, 43, 44–46; tasting notes, 47
Old Crow Distillery: brand-name litigation, 43–54; "Give 'em the Bird" litigation, 54–58; Glenn's Creek, 44–46; injury litigation, 87; at J. S. Taylor Distillery, 157n56; *Life* advertisement, 45; at

W. L. Weller & Sons, 133

Woodford Reserve Distillery: *Barton* litigation, 75–76, 139–42; bourbon revival, role in, 6; Glenn's Creek, 44–46; Pepper, Crow, and Labrot, connection to, 6, 24–25; source of bourbon, 139–42; tasting notes, Woodford Reserve Distiller's Select bourbon, 140; tasting notes, Woodford Reserve Double Oaked bourbon, 142

working conditions. *See* unsafe working conditions

World War I, temperance-inspired restrictions, 110

World War II: restrictions and suspension of production, 67, 113–14, 130; shortages and sourcing, 128–31

Wright, John J., 99

Wright & Taylor, 99, 103–4

Yantis, S. S., 65

Yellowstone bourbon, tasting notes, 69

CPSIA information can be obtained
at www.ICGtesting.com
Printed in the USA
LVHW032030040521
686493LV00001B/1